How To Cope With Difficult People

Alain Houel & Christian H. Godefroy

Contents

How To Cope With Difficult People	19
Alan Houel with Christian Godefroy	19
Foreword	21
INTRODUCTION	23
Main types of difficult people	24
Type A: Aggressive	24
Type B: Negative	25
Type C: Clams	25
There are ways to overcome these problems	26
Inner shields	26
Words as weapons	26
Negotiating ability	27
Humour	27
PART ONE **Who Are Difficult People And** **How Should You Deal With Them?**	29
CHAPTER 1 **What if others consider you a difficult person...**	31
What are we made of?	31
The image you project	31
Your personality	31
Four forces that determine your personality	32
If you were raised in a positive environment...	32

If you were raised in a cold, reserved family... 32

If your parents encouraged you... 33

If you were constantly put down... 33

Your behaviour models... 33

Your values... 33

What to look for in others? 34

Are you able to assert yourself when faced with difficult people? 34

What is your capacity for self affirmation? 35

Questionnaire: Self diagnosis 35

Comments 36

Results 37

Are you condemned to remain the prey of difficult people? 38

Quiet efficiency 38

What prevents you from being quietly efficient? 38

Questionnaire: Self evaluation 39

Results 39

How not to be a spineless bore 40

Boasting as a means of reassuring yourself 40

Accept yourself as you are 41

The keys to dealing successfully with difficult people . . 41

    1. Avoid getting upset by other people's behaviour   41

    2. Make an effort to improve your appearance . . 42

Programme: You and your appearance 42

    3. Learn to say "No" 43

    Exercise: Learning to learn to say "No" 44

CHAPTER 2
Aggressive Persons — 47

Steamroller types - What they're like... 47

Portrait No. 1 47

Portrait No. 2 47

How to behave when faced with an aggressive person? . . 49

1. Refuse to yield an inch of ground 49

2. Give the other person a chance to calm down and then place him or her in the position of having to justify his behaviour. 50

3. Look for a way to deescalate 51

An especially dangerous aggressive type: the Surgeon . 52

    Surgical incision No. 1: 52

    Surgical incision No. 2: 52

Disguised hostility 53

What strategy should you use? 54

    1. Get the aggressor with his/her back to the wall . 54

    2. Reassure the other person and then deliver your own killing blow 55

    Examples 56

A final warning 57

Don't take all shows of aggression personally 57

Your exercise programme 58

Exercise 1: Confrontation practice 59

Exercise 2: Listening to others 60

Exercise 3: Keep a journal 60

A few sample response for confrontation training 60

    1. A mother to her daughter: 61

2. A client to the assistant manager: 61

3. An adolescent to his/her father: 62

CHAPTER 3

63

What are they like? Portraits 63

Never satisfied.... 63

Defeatists... 64

Pessimists... 64

Example: 64

Forever victims... 65

A destructive influence 65

Example: 66

They may be sensitive... 66

How to help others and yourself at the same time 67

1. Find out exactly what the grievances are 67

For example: 67

Here's how you can proceed: 68

Understanding doesn't mean you're in agreement . . . 68

At all costs, avoid the "persecutor - victim - saviour" triangle 68

2. Suggest other concrete options 70

Let's look at our example... 70

3. Help people become aware of their responsibility . . 71

Ask a question 72

Set aside everything that isn't your responsibility 74

Another way to make someone assume responsibility . 75

Obeying unconscious prohibitions means being condemned to impotence 76

Example   77

    4. Last resort: get them mad! 79

    Example: 80

    Get the person to concentrate on the positive side . . . 81

    A very powerful method 82

    What to do if you feel your efforts have failed? 83

    Your training programme 83

    Transform your own history as a "victim" 84

    Root out your false obligations 85

        Use the following model: 86

CHAPTER 4
Clams   87

    What are clams like? 87

    Portrait No. 1 87

    Portrait No. 2 87

    How can you differentiate between a clam and someone who just doesn't talk much? 88

    Portrait No. 1 89

    Portrait No. 2 89

    What can we deduce from a clam's behaviour? 90

    The silence of rejection or punishment 90

    Automatic rejection mechanism 91

    The silence of protection or avoiding responsibility . . . 93

    Avoiding painful confrontation 93

    The silence of emotional repression 94

    It's healthy to be able to express our emotions 95

The silence of incomprehension and boredom 96
Do you speak the same language? 97
Three ways of perceiving the world 97
The principles of affinity 99
Six ways of sorting information 99
Dream vacations 100
Talkative one day, silent another 101
No one filter is better or worse than another 101
A few important recommendations for all clam types . . 102
1. Ask the right questions 103
Avoid "closed" questions 103
Avoid insinuating questions 104
Ask open-ended questions 104
Don't let silences embarrass you 105
Don't always try to fill the silences 106
So what should you do? 106
Try the "Suppose we..." technique 107
Example 1: 107
Example 2: 108
If nothing works... ask yourself if you're really interested
    in the person 108
Telephone clams 109
Why do telephones create clams? 109
What can you do to make them talk? 110
What to do if the person on the other end remains silent? 110
Your training programme 111
Discerning the predominant sensory input in others . . 111

What problems are involved? 112

If you can't use the test 113

Choice of words reflect the dominant sense 113

Characteristic words 114

NON-SPECIFIC: 115

Analyse a conversation to determine its V.A.S. 115

Exercise: Moving from one language to another 116

Recognising categories of information- sorting 117

If you can't use the test... 117

Adapt to the different criteria of the people around you . 118

CHAPTER 5
Verbal Ping Pong or The Dangers of Playing Offense 121

The example of the golden bracelet 121

Another example: 122

Let's take another look at our examples... 124

What are the results of this dangerous game? 125

How to remedy this problem? 126

1. Become aware of the problem 126

Exercise: Examining your subconscious 127

2. Don't allow a relationship to deteriorate 127

An example 128

3. Share your feelings 130

Say "No" without destroying a relationship 131

Take the risk of showing your vulnerability 132

People who demand perfection are difficult to live with . 132

Overcome the obstacle of resentment 133
The anatomy of resentment 134
Resentment is born of expectation 134
Who does your resentment hurt? 135
An example: 135
How to free yourself of resentment 136
Change the behaviour 136
Change the image 137

What to do when the situation has been going on for a long time?   138

Your training programme 139
Work on resentment 139
Clean up your communication act 139
Preparing for reconciliation 140
The process of forgiveness 141
Relaxation and visualisation exercise 141

PART TWO

WHAT WEAPONS DO YOU HAVE AT YOUR DISPOSAL?   149

CHAPTER 6
Four Important Stages   151

Why proceed in stages? 151
1. Calmly evaluate the situation by asking yourself some questions 152
A. Does the person always react in the same way? . . . 152

An example: 153

B. Are you over-reacting? 154

C. Will a frank discussion be enough to clear up the situation? 156

Example: 157

2. Stop trying to change other people 157

Human beings can change 157

Our wishes are not reality 158

You can influence people's attitudes 159

3. Distance yourself 159

4. Adopt a strategy and apply it 160

The upper hand 160

Avoid win - lose situations 161

Win-win strategy and the game of life 162

We have the choice 163

Become aware of negative interaction 163

Above all, strive for positive interaction 164

Conditions for the success of your strategy 165

Make sure your subject is not under any excess pressure 166

You shouldn't be under any excess pressure either . . . 167

Prepare a worst-case scenario 167

Evaluate the pro's and con's carefully 168

CHAPTER 7
The Weapon of Words: 171

Putting Them To Good Use 171

The three commandments of defence 172

1. Know how to recognise an attack 172

An example: 173

2. Adapt your defence to the kind of attack 174

3. Carry your defence strategy through to the end . . . 175

Attack: the most frequent types 176

1. Disguised accusations 176

Type B: Even... should... 177

Practical training 179

Example of Type A response: "If you really... 179

Now it's your turn: 180

Example of Type B: Even... should... 180

Your turn again: 181

2. Appealing to emotions 182

Examples 182

Practical training 183

Your turn: 184

Words as weapons: Conclusions 185

CHAPTER 8
Shields and Inner Strength   187

How to recognise the different levels of aggression . . . 187

Shows of physical aggression 187

Stay far enough away... 188

Shows of intellectual aggression 189

Shows of emotional aggression are both physical and
    mental 190

Why do we suffer? 191

Automatic suffering and how to stop it 192
Deadly gestures and phrases 192
Deadly phrases 193
On-off switches 193
Are we puppets? 194
We can change or eliminate automatic reactions 195
How to desensitise ourselves 195
How to neutralise deadly phrases 196
How to re-programme yourself 196
Mental and emotional shields 197
     We become what we think 197
Self fulfilling prophecy 198
If you want more - say it! 199
How to create effective affirmations 199
Four words to avoid 201
How to make your affirmations operational 202
Affirmations as emotional shields 203
We cannot experience two emotions or think two thoughts at the same time 204
The power of paradox 204
Attacking your self esteem 205
An infallible response 206
The power of incantations 206
An almost superhuman force 207
The power of disassociation 207
How to remain disassociated 208
Switch places 208

Visualisation exercise 210
Physical techniques for controlling emotion 214
Dynamic Relaxation 215
You have all the resources you need 215
Where do we hide our courage? 216
Visualisation : Accessing a resource 217

CHAPTER 9
The Supreme Weapon: Humour!   221

The essence of humour 221
A case in point 222
Humour can smash obsessions 223
Humour challenges conditioned ideas 224
Even bitter humour is a liberating force 224
When can we make use of humour? 225
How to sharpen your sense of humour 226
Give your laughing muscles a workout 226
Avoid bad news 227
Create an opportunity to laugh every day 228
Exercise: Cutting through the drama 229
How can humour help you say "No"? 231
    1. You gain time 231
    2. Humour prevents a loss of face 231
    3. Humour eases tension 232
    4. Humour neutralises aggressiveness 232
Let's look at an example: 233
Resist the temptation to be sarcastic! 233

    Don't make fun of other people 234

    Humour in the lion's den 234

Conclusion   236

APPENDICES   238

    Appendix To Chapter 2 Passive Aggressiveness 238

    How to deal with people who always say "Yes" but never
        keep their word 238

    How to make the person keep his / her word 238

    What to do if all this doesn't work? 239

    For example: 239

Appendix to Chapter 4 V.A.S. Test   240

    1. You have to spend six weeks locked up in an underground bomb shelter. You'll have everything necessary for your survival (water, electricity, basic foods, cot and blankets, etc.) You can only bring one singe additional item from the following list with you. Which do you choose? 240

    2. The thing you like best about a fireplace is: . . . 240

    3. You were invited to a fashionable reception. What you liked most about it was: 241

    4. You're going out for the first time with someone you find very attractive. What you like most about the person is: 241

    5. What you dislike most in a bed is: 241

    6. When giving directions to someone you tend to:
        - A6. Provide detailed verbal descriptions. . 241

8. Aside from monetary or sentimental value, the gift you'd most prefer receiving would be: . 242

9. If you wanted to relax, you'd choose: 242

10. What you find most intolerable about large, overpopulated cities is: 242

11. The thing you find most attractive about a river is: 243

12. When you think about something pleasant: . . 243

Analysis Table 243

Visual 244

Auditory 244

Tactile (Kinesthetic) 245

Olfactory or Gustatory 245

Criteria Test 245

1. Which of the following events would you find most painful? 245

2. What is it about past vacations that has made the deepest impression on your mind? . . . 246

3. You have a choice between six jobs: they all offer the same salary, vacation, tenure, and social programmes, and are situated at equal distances from your home. However, each has a particular advantage. Which would you choose? 246

4. For professional reasons, you have to leave home to spend a year in an underdeveloped, tropical country. What worries you the most is: 247

5. When you think about your childhood, what kinds of memories come most easily to mind? 248

6. Your dream is to: 248

7. The year is 1500 B.C. You are a counsellor to the Pharaoh of Egypt. You are given completely free choice to pick one item, dedicated to posterity, that will be buried with the Pharaoh in his tomb. What would you choose? 249

8. You learn about the discovery of a tribe of people hither to unknown, in a remote Himalayan valley. The first thing you want to know is: 249

Analysis Table 250

E. Events 250

P. Places 250

A. Activities 251

Pe. People 251

I. Information 251

O. Objects 252

Appendix to Chapter 7
Exercise Corrections
A few sample responses: **252**

Exercise on page 173 "If you... really..." 252

First spouse: 252

Second spouse: 252

Exercise: "Even you... should..." 254

Exercise: appealing to emotions (pg.179) 256

Credits   **257**

How To Cope With Difficult People

Alan Houel with Christian Godefroy

An expert on the subject of difficult people, Alan Houel holds an MA in sociology and communication, is a specialist in educational technology and in management psychology, and Assistant Director of the Center for Business development in Paris. For the past eight years, he has been conducting seminars on management training, communication and negotiation techniques for groups of national and multinational executives, in Europe and South America.

Christian Godefroy is a specialist in positive thinking and autosuggestion. He has given training seminars to over 6,000 senior company personnel around the world on self-confidence, communication and relaxation. Today he concentrates on publishing books about personal and professional success and about health and runs his own highly successful publishing companies in France and Switzerland.

©IAB SA

All rights reserved. No part of this book may be reproduced or transmitted in any form or by any means, electronic or mechanical, including photocopying, recording, or by any information storage and retrieval system, without permission in writing from the publisher.

ISBN ebook 978-2-37318-028-2 ISBN paper 978-2-37318-027-5

Foreword

My life would have been a lot simpler had I not met so many people with difficult personalities.

The first of these who comes to mind is my father. Ah, my father - not someone you'd call easy to get along with! He was always a terribly anxious and pessimistic person. According to him, you always had to be prepared for the worst, an attitude which often led to conflict - he discouraged me from undertaking a lot of things that I had my heart set on doing.

Also, it was almost impossible to please my father. Nothing I did was ever good enough to merit a "Congratulations son!" which would have encouraged me to keep on striving to do better.

The kind of relationship we have with our parents during childhood has a profound influence on our relationships later on in life. This is because we spend our lives trying to resolve whatever has been left unresolved in our relationship with our parents, either directly (with the parents themselves) or indirectly, with the persons who replace them in our minds.

Of course human beings are flexible enough to find thousands of ways of compensating for their childhood problems, and we will see in the chapters that follow just how this creates people who are difficult to deal with.

The research, experiments and self-analysis that I have been involved in over the last fifteen years, has enabled me to discover the secrets of developing calm and effective human relations.

I was able to understand what made my father so difficult, how to deal with him, and how to deal with all the other types of "difficult" people we meet in the course of our day to day lives.

I benefitted so much from this knowledge that I decided to change careers so that I could inform other people of my discoveries, and help them, both on a personal and professional level. So I became a lecturer, and conducted seminars on communication, human relations and personal development.

In the course of my work, I've had to work with all kinds of people who are considered very difficult to deal with by their friends, family and colleagues. But by applying my methods for bringing out the best in each person, I hardly noticed the difficult side of their personalities at all.

On the following pages you will find the secrets and methods that will enable you to do the same. Welcome and enjoy!

INTRODUCTION

There are certain recurring situation in our lives - encounters that seem to follow the same pattern - and these situations often involve so-called "difficult" people.

How many people do you know who complain bitterly about their employers, or who end up divorcing a succession of spouses after living out some sadistic and destructive drama?

"Maybe s/he'll be luckier next time," we say to ourselves, yet each time the same old story seems to repeat itself, and the relationship ends in disaster.

What about you? Have you ever had to deal with a choleric, explosive boss? A maddeningly uncooperative bureaucrat? A hostile client? An arrogant salesperson? A moody, taciturn subordinate, a grumpy colleague? An apathetic and unruly student?

If not, it's either because you live on a desert island or because you're fooling yourself. Whatever the reason, if you've never had to deal with difficult people, then you don't need to read this book.

"I can't stand Charles any more!" a biologist mutters about a colleague. "We're supposed to work together, but whenever I make a suggestion he cuts me off, treats me like some kind of ignoramus, and gets angry if I insist on making my point. Of course, as soon as my back's turned, he starts talking as if the idea were his, and if it works, he takes all the credit. He never shares. He never discusses anything, even though we're supposed to have regular meetings. I don't know what to do any more."

"I saw my father. It was a disaster," says a young man, 25 years old. "He still doesn't take me seriously. In his eyes, I'm still a kid, an ignorant kid. He contradicts everything I say, and gets angry every time we try to have a discussion. He knows it all, and I don't know anything. He'll even stick to an opinion that he knows very well is totally contradictory, just so he won't have to admit I'm right. He gets upset and starts to complain about his health, and then I feel guilty for making him feel bad."

These situations, and thousands of others like them, are commonplace. Unfortunately, they result in a lot of anxiety, exasperation and frustration.

How easy life would be if we didn't have to deal with difficult people! Relationships would be harmonious, and there would be more justice and tolerance in the world.

But is there something we could do to get what we want, even from difficult people? Are there any secrets for making human relations harmonious and effective, however difficult people appear to be?

Whether we're talking about day to day life, or about our personal or intimate relationships, or about the family or about work, it's always useful to know how to deal with difficult people in order to communicate, and live side by side as best as possible.

By harmonising our relations, we assert ourselves and develop our own personality, while at the same time allowing others to do the same.

Main types of difficult people

Studies conducted in the United States have indicated that people qualified as "difficult to deal with" can be categorised into a few main types. In other words, the same types of people always seem to cause the problems.

We will begin with an analysis of these types. You'll quickly realise that you've been dealing with some of them on a regular basis.

Type A: Aggressive

First, aggressivity. This category includes various behaviours such as hostility, the desire to hurt, being sarcastic, refusing to cooperate, arrogance and a "know-it-all" attitude.

This type of person tries to dominate, will not hesitate to resort to insult and, contrary to popular belief about such explosive characters (their bark is worse than their bite) will not hesitate to stab you in the back if doing so serves their interests.

These people are also self-appointed experts who, because of their pride, refuse to admit that they may not know all there is to know about a given subject.

The two examples we cited earlier of difficult people fall into this category, which we will analyse first.

Type B: Negative

You're familiar with the complainers, grouches, and other negative types - there are sure to be a few among the people you know. According to these people, the only thing life has to offer is bad luck.

The principle characteristic of such people is that they love to complain. So don't expect them to find any solutions for their miseries, because in so doing they would eliminate their primary reason for living!

This category includes people whose only mission seems to be to throw a bucket of cold water on anyone who demonstrates the least enthusiasm for anything.

The problem with these kinds of people is that their attitude is toxic. Their "illness" is contagious, and therefore dangerous.

Type C: Clams

Finally, this third type consists of a particular form of invertebrate - clams - who either say nothing, or at best talk about the weather, without ever really saying what they think or feel.

Clams are people who must have been inordinately impressed when their high school history teachers covered the subject of that ancient Spartan who, rather than betray the presence of his pet fox, allowed the animal, who was hidden under his cloak, to devour his intestines.

Such people usually limit their communication to grunts and groans. On a particularly good day, you may, if you're lucky, get a yes or a no out of them.

There are ways to overcome these problems

Don't get discouraged if you regularly seem to be confronted with difficult people. There are a number of methods available for dealing with these kinds of situations, depending on the type of person it is, and especially on what you hope to obtain from the dialogue.

You can reach your objectives, without resorting to force. You have a number of weapons at your disposal, whose effectiveness will astonish you, once you learn how to use them.

Inner shields

The first condition for successfully dealing with difficult people is to make yourself impermeable to their attempts to disrupt communication. The difference between someone who is vulnerable and someone who appears indestructible, is the latter's ability to construct inner shields. Here are a few pointers on how this can be done.

Words as weapons

Whether to defend yourself or support your point of view, you can learn to use words skillfully and make them your ally. We'll be looking at the principles of using words effectively later on.

Negotiating ability

Negotiating is an art, and only a few diplomats and entrepreneurs excel at it. Yet your daily life can be seen as a succession of transactions, which are open to negotiation. We'll show you how to come out a winner in your transactions with difficult people, without arousing any suspicions or feelings of abuse.

Humour

Finally, you'll learn how to develop your sense of humour, which can be a powerful weapon. You can use humour to take the drama out of a situation and to temper your own aggressive feelings. Without laughter, mankind would long ago have sunk to untold depths of misery and despair. Humour can help you deal with a host of difficult situations - it can defuse a lot of bombs, and get you out of many a lion's den without a scratch.

PART ONE
Who Are Difficult People And How Should You Deal With Them?

CHAPTER 1
What if others consider you a difficult person...

What are we made of?

You enter a room full of people. Conversation stops, and heads turn your way. People recognise you, say hello, some come up smiling and shake your hand, others get on with their discussions. You walk around, then stop to chat with an acquaintance.

A scene as banal as this one nevertheless depends on two elements which are interdependent, and which form your personality, i.e. YOUR SELF.

The image you project

The first of these elements is the image you project through your physical appearance, clothes, makeup, hairstyle, posture, facial expression, eyes, voice, handshake and gestures.

Your personality

After the image comes something that can be called personality. This is a dimension of your self that is much more difficult to pinpoint than your image. In theory, your image should simply be a reflection of your personality.

But you know very well that this usually isn't the case!

Anyone can modify their image, more or less successfully. In general, we try to present as favourable and flattering an image of ourselves as possible to the outside world. Therefore, you should never rely entirely on image to judge a person's personality. The two can be diametrically opposed.

True, this is easier said than done. And when we have nothing to go by except a person's image, it's very difficult to make anything more than a superficial judgment of a person.

Four forces that determine your personality

Your personality is made up of a myriad of complex factors which still haven't been fully identified by psychologists, and which are regularly the subject of ferocious controversy. Nevertheless, it is important to know that there are four main kinds of forces that combine to determine personality: your emotional needs, your economic needs, your values and the models you choose for yourself.

If you were raised in a positive environment...

If you were raised in a warm and loving atmosphere, then you're more likely to expect other people to like you, and you are never stingy with your own affection. Similarly, if you were raised in an economically privileged environment, then you're much less likely to become a miser with the money you earn yourself.

If you were raised in a cold, reserved family...

Careful! Just because you were raised in a family that did not demonstrate much affection doesn't mean you're incapable of feeling or expressing love. It just means you may find it more difficult to love yourself and others.

Neither does this mean that because you earned your money with the sweat off your brow and were poor as a child, that you automatically become a miser. Far from it! But your attitude towards the privileged classes is likely to differ from that of a person born with a silver spoon in his / her mouth.

If your parents encouraged you...

If you were always encouraged and supported in your endeavours, whatever they may have been, then you probably have a good measure of self confidence. You know your worth, you're aware of your intellectual capacities, and you certainly don't fall into the category of perpetual victims.

If you were constantly put down...

On the other hand, if the people who were important in your life always put you down and treated you like some kind of adolescent retard, or had absolutely no faith in your intellectual ability, then you probably make a perfect victim for "difficult" people. You have trouble asserting yourself, and you always try to appear above the situation, without necessarily succeeding.

Your behaviour models...

The models you choose for yourself, either consciously or unconsciously, also exercise an important influence on the way you behave. In early childhood, you probably modelled yourself after one of your parents, and unconsciously imitated him or her. A little later on, you may have chosen a friend, or a teacher with whom you had a close relationship, or a famous personality, or a colleague, a superior, a partner, etc.

Your values...

Your values are the fourth major force in your life. They are formed by your education, your environment, your studies, your job, your travels and, of course, by your religious convictions and your conception of right and wrong.

What to look for in others?

Naturally what applies to you applies to others as well. So when you find yourself confronted with a person you judge "difficult", or when you want to extricate yourself from a pointless discussion, or defend yourself against a verbal attack, first try to understand the global character of the other person. Try to lift a corner of the veil that hides his or her personality by analysing a sample of his behaviour. Don't be fooled by the person's image.

A gentle smile may conceal an iron will, while a person who appears to be high strung may also be easily influenced. Your task is to detect the person's real personality and adapt your strategy accordingly.

Are you able to assert yourself when faced with difficult people?

This point is very important. Evaluating your capacity for self assertion will dictate how you orient your "training." Do you often feel the need to justify yourself, or to enhance the image you project to others? Or are you particularly well endowed in this area?

The following exercise will help you make an honest evaluation of yourself. Don't think for a moment that this is some kind of gratuitous exercise in self punishment! To have a reasonable discussion with a difficult person, you must know how to assert yourself, and you must also be aware of your weak points, so that you can protect yourself. The people you judge to be "difficult" may not be considered so by others. Don't forget that objectivity is a word which doesn't exist in the vocabulary of human relations.

What is your capacity for self affirmation?

Questionnaire: Self diagnosis

Answer the following questions with a simple yes or no. Then give yourself 1 point for each correct response, and read the commentary.

1. Do you believe that other people are straightforward and honest with you?
   [ ] YES [ ] NO

2. Are you able to laugh about yourself?
   [ ] YES [ ] NO

3. Are you able to list 5 people who had a strong influence, either positive or negative, on your life?
   [ ] YES [ ] NO

4. Do you consider yourself to be honest towards others?
   [ ] YES [ ] NO

5. Do you think it's a good idea to enumerate your faults and qualities?
   [ ] YES [ ] NO

6. Are you interested in analysing yourself, your life, your activities, your performance at work, your personal relations, etc.?
   [ ] YES [ ] NO

7. Are you often disappointed by others?
   [ ] YES [ ] NO

8. Do you think that total control of our emotions is possible - and desirable - in order to assert ourselves?
   [ ] YES [ ] NO

Comments

Now look at each question and circle your correct responses.

1. YES. It is important that others be honest with you. Even though the truth isn't always pleasant to hear, it is an important step on the road to maturity and self affirmation. If you're under the impression that people around you are afraid of telling you the truth, then you are probably one of those "difficult" people who make human relations such a sticky business!

2. YES. Most eminent psychologists agree on this point. Being able to laugh about yourself means that you know yourself, and that you can judge yourself without resentment.

3. YES. We're all influenced by other people in one way or another. If you answered in the negative, then you're not being honest with yourself. You refuse to recognise the influence of the people you associate with, and it's possible that you fall into one of the categories of "difficult" people, either the aggressive type or the know-it-all (see Chapter 2). Take the time to draw up a list of people who influence you - it's an excellent exercise.

4. YES. If you insist on people being honest with you, then the least you can do is return the favour.

5. YES. Make two lists: one of your qualities and one of your faults. Then ask someone who knows you well, and whose judgment you respect, for his o r her opinion. If you can't think of anyone to ask, it may be a sign that you're not completely honest with yourself.

6. YES. If you aren't, then you may wake up one day to find that your life has lost its meaning, that you live to work instead of work to live, that your personal relations have lost their spark and become simple habits, etc.

7. NO. Of course we are occasionally disappointed by others, but we should always ask ourselves if we're not trying to shift the blame onto someone else's shoulders, or if we see ourselves as we really are.

8. NO. It's neither realistic nor healthy to spend your time trying to master your emotions. Among other things, you lose contact with yourself. For example, if you know that a given situation irritates you, you'd try to avoid it. On the other hand, if you recognise your need for affection and satisfaction, then you should try to fill this need. You will become a more fulfilled person, whom others will want to know.

Results

- Between 0 and 2: You don't see yourself as you are. Other people probably find you hard to deal with. You will not be able to assert yourself, or become a fulfilled person, or gain the upper hand when dealing with difficult people, if you don't reconcile the way you see yourself with the way you really are. You clearly need to read this book, and apply the methods it contains!

- Between 3 and 5: You have certain moments of lucidity. Unfortunately, you don't take the time to evaluate yourself seriously. Make the effort - success is at your doorstep.

- Between 5 and 8: You know yourself, you're honest with yourself and you're probably honest with others as well. You will need only a minimum of effort to learn how to deal successfully with difficult people. You are mature, and you're prepared to accept what life has to offer - happiness and sadness, joy, success and failure.

Are you condemned to remain the prey of difficult people?

As you've probably noticed, some people never complain about others. For them, there's no such thing as a difficult person. They seem to have a great talent for human relations, and are surrounded by people who visibly demonstrate great affection and admiration for them. These privileged persons always seem to know exactly what to say to resolve unpleasant situations, and they are able to tame the fiercest of demons.

Of course, these people also usually obtain what they want, without arousing any antagonism or resentment - people continue to like and respect them.

Why are they gifted in this way, and more importantly HOW do they do it?

Quiet efficiency

Such persons have the innate or acquired ability to instil all their interpersonal relations with a kind of quiet efficiency. They are confident and fulfilled, and fear neither the rejection or hostility of others. Consequently, they know how to defend themselves against verbal attack, and negotiate in a way that allows them to come out on top, and effortlessly dominate a situation, while never having to justify themselves.

Are you already a member of this privileged group, or do you still have to put up with "difficult" people?

What prevents you from being quietly efficient?

If you're not sure of the answer, complete the following test by answering the questions with a simple yes or no:

Questionnaire: Self evaluation

1. Are you in the habit of talking about your accomplishments, either professional or other, in order to impress people?
   [ ] YES [ ] NO

2. Do you have trouble saying no to people?
   [ ] YES [ ] NO

3. When you think about your spouse, do you tend to think that s/he doesn't understand you?
   [ ] YES [ ] NO

4. Are you easily influenced by other people's bad moods or depressions?
   [ ] YES [ ] NO

5. Do you find it difficult to satisfy your need to be alone or private without feeling guilty?
   [ ] YES [ ] NO

6. Do you have trouble distancing yourself from people whom you find boring or unpleasant?
   [ ] YES [ ] NO

7. Do you tend to constantly justify yourself?
   [ ] YES [ ] NO

Results

Each affirmative response represents one aspect of your behaviour that you should work on. If you don't, you'll continue to fall prey to annoying, bad-tempered, hostile, moody, and other types of difficult people. For them, you are a perfect victim. They consider you a weak person, and this makes the task of upsetting you a lot easier.

We all need moments of calm and solitude, when we can just sit down and think about things. If you feel you have to justify yourself every time you decide to spend some time on your own, then the benefits of that time alone will be greatly diminished. Remember that privacy is every person's absolute right, and that insisting on your own privacy now and then is a good occasion to exercise your rights.

How not to be a spineless bore

David is a stock broker who lost his job a year ago, when the company he was working for was bought out by a large corporation. He hasn't been able to find another job since then. Every time he goes to a job interview something happens - he immediately feels an instinctive dislike for the person sitting across the table, and loses all his self confidence.

When he tried to contact old business acquaintances to see if they could do something for him, they all seemed embarrassed and eager to escape as quickly as possible, even before he'd have a chance to ask for their support. David was on the verge of depression.

Boasting as a means of reassuring yourself

A few sessions with a personal development counsellor opened his eyes to a lot of things. He understood that he alone was responsible for his situation. Lacking self assurance and confidence, he felt a constant need to reassure himself by boasting, name dropping, and annoying his listeners with exaggerated accounts o f his exploits.

Unfortunately, no one was taken in, and David became a victim of his own lack of self love and of his feelings of inferiority. This went on until even his close friends and family found him hard to take. No wonder he didn't do well in his job interviews!

Accept yourself as you are

If you want to assert yourself so that you can come out a winner in your encounters with "difficult" people, then you have to learn to accept yourself as you are, and stop trying to constantly build yourself up. If not, you will soon be considered hard to get along with by others and, like David, you will be ostracised by your peers.

If you want to maintain fruitful relations with others, heed the following advice. Because the first condition for success is to stop communicating from a position of inferiority.

The keys to dealing successfully with difficult people

1. Avoid getting upset by other people's behaviour

If you find somebody's behaviour shocking, ignore it, especially if you're not directly involved. By showing your outrage, you adopt the attitude of a victim. You automatically place yourself in an inferior position. If you allow yourself to be manipulated on an emotional level, you will not be able to gain the upper hand when confronting difficult people.

Whenever you feel irritated by the attitudes of people who have no real influence on your life, just shrug it off. Learn to say, "So what?" to yourself, and forget it.

Exercise: How to develop serenity and self confidence

- For the next few days, write down any events, words, attitudes or other behaviour which you find shocking or insulting. Write down everything, even if it seems insignificant: an encounter with a road hog, or someone who slams a door, for example.

- Analyse each event, and objectively determine to what degree your attitude worked in your favour. Be completely honest with yourself.

- As the exercise gradually becomes part of your daily routine, you'll notice that you're less affected by events which you previously found outrageous or disconcerting. You will acquire more self confidence and a sense of inner serenity, and your blood pressure will go down!

2. Make an effort to improve your appearance

You're probably aware that as far as human relations go, the first few minutes of contact are decisive in determining the future of the relationship. The first characteristic upon which you judge other people is their appearance. Despite all our objections, and even though we know that appearances are often deceptive, it remains an undeniable fact that many relationships are either pursued or abandoned because of appearance.

Also, appearance is an important factor in developing a healthy dose of self esteem. You will be less likely to assume the role of a victim if you are well groomed, if you create the impression that you're someone who takes care of yourself and, without being childishly vain, feel good about your physical appearance. We repeat: you have no chance of coming out on top in your encounters with difficult people if you show any signs of inferiority right at the start.

Programme: You and your appearance

What do you think about the way you look now? Make a list of what you like and don't like about yourself:

- I like:

- I don't like:

Now try to find ways to enhance your positive aspects, and diminish your negative ones:

- What to enhance:

- What to diminish:

Are your clothes right for you? If you're not sure you have good taste, ask for advice. You must know someone who is supposed to have good taste. You'll flatter the person by asking, and s/he will be only too happy to help you. As a bonus, you may gain a friend, as well as some good advice about clothes.

3. Learn to say "No"

In life, it's much harder to say no than to say yes. Admit it - you've often said yeas when you wanted to say no!

For example, say you have to work overtime on a night you're supposed to go out with your spouse. But you don't dare say no to your boss. Or you agree to babysit for a friend on Saturday night, when you'd really prefer to do something on your own. And so on...

And each time you say it won't happen again.

Fear of rejection Fear of rejection, which is the motivating force behind the incapacity to say no, is easy to understand. Psychologists agree that this fear does not correspond to any real threat. You don't lose a friend's affection or respect just because you diplomatically refuse to do something for him or her. If this does happen, then just tell yourself that the person did not merit any of YOUR affection, and even less of YOUR respect, in the first place!

Always saying yes when you really want to refuse will make you bitter and cause you unnecessary stress. If you want to affirm yourself and deal successfully with difficult situations, then you must learn to say no, tactfully, politely and gently - but also firmly. You'll be respected all the more for it, and you may be astonished to discover that people whom you previously found "difficult" become easier and easier to handle.

Exercise: Learning to learn to say "No"

For each of the following situations, you will find three negative answers. Choose the one which you think is best:

1. Your mother-in-law calls you and wants you to take her shopping on a Saturday afternoon. You would prefer staying home. You respond by saying:

   a. "I'm really sorry, but I have a dentist's appointment. (This is just an excuse - you don't really have an appointment.)

   b. I don't feel like shopping. I find it boring, and I have more important things to do.

   c. Would you mind if we postponed it for another afternoon? I really feel like I need to rest up this weekend.

2. At the end of an exhausting day, your boss asks you to take some files home and study them that night. You say:

   a. "Really, I have better things to do with my evenings!"

   b. You make up some excuse.

c. "I'm too tired to do any useful work this evening. What if I do it on Saturday morning instead?"

3. Your spouse invites someone over for dinner whom you can't stand. You say:

a. "Alright, we'll let it go this time, but next time tell me in advance so I can make other plans."

b. You agree to entertain the person because you're afraid of displeasing your spouse.

c. You go out yourself, and let your spouse entertain the guest alone.

Answers:

1. The best answer is C. It can be dangerous to invent excuses, since you may be found out later on, especially if you're dealing with someone you see frequently. The second response is tactless, and borders on being rude. Your mother-in-law would probably feel offended by it.

2. Once again, the best response is C, for the same reasons as the preceding question.

3. Here the best response is A. You calmly make your position clear, while agreeing to the invitation one last time. You could also opt for the last response, i.e. leaving your spouse alone with the guest. That way everyone will probably have a better time, you included!

Practice this exercise. Become aware of similar situations that are likely to arise in your own life, and make a list of possible negative responses. Little by little you'll learn to say "No" without being afraid of appearing callous and uncaring.

CHAPTER 2
Aggressive Persons

Steamroller types - What they're like...

Portrait No. 1

"I'm so sorry, sir," explains the salesperson, "but your guaranty has been invalid for a few months. Anyway, I don't see how you can blame the fact that your toaster isn't working properly on faulty production. You probably did something, maybe when you were transporting it..."

"What! Is this supposed to be some kind of joke!" the client replies angrily. "What kind of store is this! You sell defective items and then you won't even admit it! And you have the nerve to call me a liar!"

"Not at all, sir. Try to calm down," mumbles the salesperson. "That's not what I was trying to say..."

"Ha! I know very well what you were trying to say," the client interrupts. "I want to talk to the manager. At least he may be a little more competent than you..."

Portrait No. 2

"This presentation is a disaster," groans the Vice President, looking over sketches for an ad campaign. "The client will never approve it."

"A disaster!" the Art Director in charge of the project exclaims indignantly. "What are you talking about? We think it's just fine, and we came in under budget. Everybody thinks it's great."

"Everybody? Who's everybody? You mean the group of idiots I have working for me? I can't delegate anything. You're not even capable of making a decent presentation!"

"But sir," the Art Director sputters, "we followed all your directions and..."

"Get out of here before I get really mad. And do this thing again!"

When we talk about "difficult" people, we are primarily referring to aggressive, hostile, arrogant types - nicknamed steamrollers - described in the two portraits you've just read. If they seem exaggerated, it's not by much.

People who fall into this category often seem to take issue not only with your behaviour or your reactions, but also with YOU as a person. They seem to be accusing you for just existing, and you may end up believing that they dislike or even hate you, and that they have the right to verbally brutalise you because of their superior position.

When they discover just how much they can terrorise and humiliate their victims, such aggressive types, as soon as they find themselves in a position of authority (exactly like the client or the Vice President described above) count on the effects their behaviour produces in other people: mental confusion, stuttering, blushing, sweating, trembling, tears, etc.

Such reactions don't do much to put an aggressive person in his or her place. So the steamroller keeps on rolling, crushing everything in its path.

People with dominating, antagonistic characters are very hard to live and work with, both to the people around them, and to themselves. They're often angry, and are rarely able to share moments of simple pleasure.

Since they're not always able to express their aggressiveness, they start imagining violent scenes where they can exact the revenge they crave. The only way they feel they can get something from another person is through threats and violent criticism.

When in danger, they react brutally and automatically, and are incapable of reasoning things out. This often works to their disadvantage, and can even place their survival in jeopardy.

How to behave when faced with an aggressive person?

In situations similar to the ones we've just described, you should adopt a strategy which has two main elements:

1. Refuse to yield an inch of ground

In fact, aggressive persons have a clear idea of how their behaviour is going to affect you, since they're in the habit of intimidating others, and by so doing, getting what they want. Therefore, if you stand up to their insults and shows of hostility, you will throw them off track.

They know off by heart the little scene that is supposed to unfold, resulting in their obtaining what they want. If you refuse to play along with their scenario, they'll freeze up sooner or later. And that's when you can take control of the situation and suggest a more acceptable attitude.

Example:

Let's take another look at the first scenario.

"What! Are you trying to make fun of me?" the client replies angrily. "What kind of store is this! You sell defective items and then you won't even admit it! And you have the nerve to call me a liar!"

"Not at all, sir," replies the salesperson, calmly but firmly. "You misunderstood me. If you'd care to leave your toaster with us, we'll call you as soon as we find out what's wrong with it, and give you an estimate for the repairs. If that's not satisfactory, perhaps you'd care to talk to the manager?"

Now the situation is turned around. The salesperson has removed any grounds for hostility:

- 1) By refusing to get upset or defensive, the aggressive client's insults just evaporate into thin air.

- 2) By suggesting a simple and logical line of action, the salesperson keeps the discussion in a realistic framework.

- 3) By suggesting a meeting with the manager, the client is forced to think twice. If there were any blame or guilt in the matter, would the salesperson suggest a meeting with the manager? Probably not. Also, the manager is much less likely to be intimidated than the sales person.

All the client can do is accept the solution suggested by the salesperson, or take the toaster and leave. In both cases, the salesperson remains in control of the situation.

2. Give the other person a chance to calm down and then place him or her in the position of having to justify his behaviour.

It is sometimes impossible to react by remaining totally indifferent when an aggressive person explodes or intimidates you. But to avoid adding fuel to the fire, you must give the person an opportunity to calm down. Then oblige the person to justify his or her behaviour.

For example:

Let's look at the second situation described above:

"This presentation is a disaster," groans the Vice President, looking over sketches for an ad campaign. "The client will never approve it."

"Why not?" the Art Director calmly asks.

"Why? It's obvious! Even YOU should be able to see that it will never work!"

"Exactly, and I'd be very happy if you could explain in detail why YOU think the campaign is a failure, and especially why you think the client won't approve it. You have much more experience than we do. Take your time. I'll get us some coffee..."

Once again a bomb has been defused. The Art Director, without in any way demeaning himself:

- 1) Forced the V.P. to justify his anger and his negative opinion of the project.

- 2) Did not get upset, at least not outwardly, by the sarcasm in the statement... "Even YOU can see why it won't work..." even though this kind of remark is extremely negative and is meant solely to hurt someone.

- 3) Gave the V.P. a chance to cool off by going to get coffee. If the V.P. persists in being aggressive after that, he'll just look like a fool, especially if the Art Director remains calm. And aggressive persons don't like to appear foolish, any more than anyone else.

3. Look for a way to deescalate

If you're dealing with a steamroller personality, you must at all costs look for a way to deescalate the situation. If you respond to hostility with an equally hostile attitude, you'll only fall into a trap and feed their aggressiveness. Aggressive people take pleasure in opposition or antagonism - that's when they feel they are living with the greatest intensity.

But if you can find a way to agree with the position of someone who systematically disagrees with everything, then that person will become disoriented, because in order to disagree with you s/he will have to disagree with himself!

When my son was three years old, he represented a perfect example of this kind of behaviour. There are stages in children's development that are called "phases of opposition." Learning to assert yourself in the world, and especially in relation to adults, takes the form of systematically negating everything that is asked or suggested:

"Do you want chicken or hamburgers for supper?"

"I don't want anything!"

"Well, if that's the way you want to be, you'll have chicken like everyone else, and you won't get any dessert until you finish!"

- Child starts crying and shouting, etc.

"Get to your room! You're going to bed... "But I'm not tired!"

"Put your pyjamas on, the blue ones." "No! I want the red ones..."

And so on. If you have children, you know what I'm talking about. If you still have children, then try to find a way to agree with the child, instead of opposing him / her.

When he says, "I don't want to eat anything..." just answer, "All right, you won't eat anything..." You'll be surprised a moment later when he does an about face and demands something to eat (because he wants to disagree with you again) which is exactly what you wanted in the first place, isn't it?

An especially dangerous aggressive type: the Surgeon

Surgical incision No. 1:

"From what I know of your husband, he's not the type to sit around moping while you're away," says a geologist to his female colleague while on a field trip that's due to last several weeks.

Surgical incision No. 2:

"It doesn't surprise me in the least that you can't change a tire," says a husband to his wife. "Why should you be any different than any other woman?"

These kinds of statements are par for the course with surgical aggressive types. They take pleasure in cutting you to the quick, and then go ahead and dig the knife in some more.

Their incisive remarks assume many forms: more or less subtle double meanings, sarcasm, jokes at the expense of a third person, etc. This kind of disguised verbal aggression is a conscious attempt to wound and maim someone psychologically.

For example, while one person in a group is expressing an opinion, the surgical aggressive type is the one who tries to catch your attention, rolling his / her eyes in disgust.

Remind you of anyone you know?

Disguised hostility

Actually, not all aggressive types express thei r hostility openly, as steamroller types do. People who disguise their hostility and create a false impression by pretending to be friendly at first, are much more dangerous.

These people specialise in making cutting remarks. They prefer more subtle methods of attack because in reality they are cowards. They never dare to be openly aggressive with someone, because they are afraid the other person may get angry, and in turn resort to aggression in order to defend him or herself.

However, by being hypocritical, they can always argue that they didn't mean any harm... that they didn't do it on purpose... that they've been misunderstood, etc. In this way they avoid having to confront any hostility head on. And this is precisely what makes them vulnerable, as we'll see a little later. However, before such people are found out, they usually succeed in doing a lot of damage. This is partly due to the fact that in their plots and machinations, they are usually able to find a third person to help them out, someone who shares their desire to cause harm, or who is simply afraid to resist, and who remains a silent witness to the aggressor's destructive stratagems.

Surgical aggressors speak in quiet tones, often accompanied by a slight smile. But inside they take great pleasure either in their victim's passive suffering, or in his / her confused emotional reaction, which outwardly seem disproportionate to the remark that triggered it off - usually just a phrase or simple gesture - which nevertheless has cut right to the heart of the victim.

This is why you usually don't have a choice when dealing with this type of person. Surgical aggressors are notorious cowards. They don't deserve your compassion. They are perfectly aware of the harm they coldly perpetrate on people whom they consider vulnerable. You must counter attack. Set your scruples aside and assert yourself. Don't let yourself become a scapegoat.

What strategy should you use?

In general you have two strategies to choose from, one being as effective as the other. It all depends on what you know about the aggressor. It's up to you to find the hole in his / her armour. Both strategies require a great degree of self control, because a cutting remark can hurt a lot more than the explosive insults of a steamroller type.

1. Get the aggressor with his/her back to the wall

Let's see what our lady geologist could have done to refute her colleague's cutting remark.

"From what I know of your husband, he's not the type to sit around moping while you're away," says a geologist to his colleague while on a field trip that's due to last several weeks.

"You're right about that. He's full of energy. He's got the garage to paint, and the kid's room needs new furniture."

In principle, this should be enough to get the aggressor to shut up. However, s/he may insist, saying something like, "That's not what I meant..."

"Really? Well what exactly do you mean?"

Now the aggressor is cornered. S/he has to come out in the open, which is precisely what these people can't stand doing, and which is why they always resort to underhanded attacks. They'll either change the subject of conversation or try to get out of it by making a joke. No one is taken in by this tactic, but it's best to be magnanimous and let it go.

Let's look at the second example:

"It doesn't surprise me in the least that you couldn't change a tire," says a husband to his wife. "Why should you be any different than mostwomen?"

The wife can counter by saying something like, "Do you think so. That's interesting. Let's discuss this. Come here and sit down. I find this fascinating. I could talk about it all day, couldn't you?"

The husband will suddenly remember a thousand things he has to do, and will leave without pursuing the argument, since his vicious little attack was disarmed so effectively.

2. Reassure the other person and then deliver your own killing blow

This manoeuvre is carried out in two steps. The first consists of treating the attack in an impersonal manner. This is the surest way to gain a victory. If you are confronting an expert in surgical aggression, it will allow you to:

- 1) Take a time-out before counter attacking.
- 2) Regain control of your emotions (provoking an emotional response is one of the ways your adversary scores points).
- 3) Deprive the aggressor of any kind of satisfaction, sine the remark, instead of cutting you to the quick, doesn't seem to bother you at all.

What could be more frustrating for an aggressor than to be suddenly faced with a feelingless robot instead of an emotional victim who is easily manipulated?

You don't have to leave the scene - you can stay where you are. Your attitude is enough to cower the aggressor into submission. However, if the cutting remark was especially nasty, or if you feel you have to take a stand once and for all with this person, then you can use your advantage to launch a final blow at your fleeing adversary.

Let's look at how this could work in practice:

Examples

"From what I know of your husband, he's not the type to sit around moping while you're away," says a geologist to his colleague while on a field trip that's due to last several weeks.

The colleague replies:

"The theory that all men start chasing skirts as soon as their wives turn their backs for a moment originated in the ramblings of a frustrated libido, which couldn't accept the success of its female counterpart, and sought ways to gain revenge on all women. Do you fall into that category?"

The tables are turned - the aggressor is now on the defensive. If s/he chooses to continue the discussion, s/he risks being forced into providing lengthy and convoluted explanations of an outdated, macho or racist attitude.

Let's look at the second example:

"It doesn't surprise me in the least that you couldn't change a tire," says a husband to his wife. "Why should you be any different than most women?"

"The concept of women as being somehow inferior seems to be prevalent among older men, especially those who are insecure about their intellectual abilities, as well as other kinds of abilities.

But I'm surprised to hear something like that coming f rom you, dear!"

And there you are - the husband will not be likely to repeat the same kind of attack in the near future.

A final warning

Before putting the strategies you've learned for dealing with steamroller and surgical aggressive types into practice in your everyday life, make sure that you're really confronted with a show of hostility. Does this seem obvious? Well, it isn't.

This is because people who are not difficult themselves, and who possess a minimum of aggressiveness, can be easily fooled by appearances. Everyone has their own way of expressing themselves. So before getting irritated by the behaviour of a person you've judged - perhaps too hastily - to be hostile or aggressive, ask yourself a few questions:

- How do other people react to this person's behaviour?
- Can this person's behaviour be justified, even though it's different from the way I'd act under identical circumstances? After all, it's perfectly normal to tell an impolite office worker or salesperson that you find their attitude unacceptable.
- Is the hostile person just playing a role in order to get what s/he wants?
- Is the person just using the occasion to let off some steam?

Don't take all shows of aggression personally

Making these distinctions is of capital importance, because if you can't differentiate between real aggression and behaviour which has nothing to do with you, you risk provoking hostility which will then be very difficult to control.

Take the example of a female lawyer who's spent a trying day in court, and who comes home at night only to find that for some reason her husband hasn't prepared dinner. Her nerves are on edge, she's exhausted, but her professional training prevents her from venting her dissatisfaction on colleagues and superiors. Instead, she attacks her husband.

"What! You haven't made dinner yet? The children must be starving! You men are all alike - can't wash a spoon without breaking a glass. God, what a day I've had! And all you can think about is watching that damn game on TV and reading your damn newspaper, while I have to do everything... etc." (This kind of invective may last for quite a while.)

Now if the husband doesn't understand that his wife's hostility is due to the difficult day she had at work, then he will respond aggressively in turn, and an all out conflict will develop, with wounds inflicted on both sides.

So countering another person's aggressiveness is a delicate operation. Make sure the measures you take are necessary. If not, you risk destroying or harming a relationship that is important to you.

Your exercise programme

If you want to acquire the habit of reacting correctly when faced with aggressive persons, either of the steamroller or surgical type, then you have to practice. Being able to come up with just the right remark, to stay calm and to avoid getting into futile arguments, isn't something you can learn from one day to the next.

Exercise 1: Confrontation practice

Complete one of the following discussions each day, using the techniques you've just learned. You should come up with at least three or four response variations for each discussion. We'll provide you with some examples of acceptable responses at the end of the chapter.

Keep inventing new responses - the possibilities are infinite.

1. A mother to her daughter:

"Really, if you had any respect for me, you wouldn't dress like up like a slut whenever I take you somewhere!"

Your response:

2. A client to the assistant manager:

"And you're telling me he's not here? That His Highness the Manager isn't around? After I've come 200 miles to see him! You knew I was coming this morning, and you couldn't even tell him? How can an idiot like you still find a job! I'm telling you that the president of this company is going to hear from me, you can bet on it. And I'll have something to say to him about you..."

Your response:

3. An adolescent to his/her father:

"Really, Dad, even you should be able to make an effort to understand that I need the car at least one night a week!"

Your response:

Exercise 2: Listening to others

Keep a small notebook with you at all times and listen to the conversations around you - while you're on the bus, train, at the post office, at the bank, in stores or offices, etc.

Whenever you overhear an aggressive person, either a steamroller or surgical type, write down what s/he says. Then, when you have some free time, complete the discussion as if you were the object of aggression, applying the techniques you've learned.

Exercise 3: Keep a journal

When we're pestered by an aggressive person, it's often only much later that we think of a remark we could have used to put the person in his/her place. So keep a journal of the discussions you have with difficult and/or aggressive people. You can use the following model:

Place and date:
Situation:
First round:
1- What the other person said:
2- How I replied:
3- How I SHOULD HAVE REPLIED:
Second round:
1- What the other person said:
2- How I replied:
3- How I SHOULD HAVE REPLIED:

A few sample response for confrontation training

Always avoid replying in a sarcastic or ironic tone.

1. A mother to her daughter:

"Really, if you had any respect for me, you wouldn't dress like up like a slut whenever I take you somewhere!"

Possible responses:

"Listen mother, where did you get the idea that I don't respect you?

Or...

"This idea of respect is very interesting. Let's talk about it some more..."

Or...

"Why do you think that I don't respect you?"

2. A client to the assistant manager:

"And you're telling me he's not here? That the His Highness the Manager isn't around? After I've come 200 miles to see him! You knew I was coming this morning, and you couldn't even tell him? How can an idiot like you still find a job! I'm telling you that the president of this company is going to hear from me, you can bet on it. And I'll have something to say to him about you..."

Possible responses:

"Sir, I did give your letter to the manager. Now, if you want to make a complaint to the President of the company, I'll be happy to give you his name and address. But maybe I could first explain why the manager is unable to see you today?"

Or...

"Sir, I feel terrible that you've had to travel all this way for nothing, but if you ask your secretary, you'll see that we tried to reach you this morning, when the manager found out he had to take care of an emergency. Now, if you want to file a complaint with the President, I'll be happy to... (see previous response)."

3. An adolescent to his/her father:

"Really, Dad, even you should be able to make an effort to understand that I need the car at least one night a week!"

Possible responses:

"Are you trying to tell me that I'm different from all your friends' fathers? Maybe we could discuss it, if you have a moment? I'm interested to know exactly what you think about me."

Or...

"It's natural for adolescents to think that everyone is ganged up against them. Would you like to talk about it some more?"

Or...

"Adolescents who aren't very evolved seem to think that the only reason their parents exist is to say no. I didn't think you fell into that category."

CHAPTER 3

What are they like? Portraits

"I know you live pretty far away, Martin, but it's important for the work we're doing here that you get to work on time in the morning. I'd really appreciate it if you made an effort to do so."

"What else would you appreciate? You put the entire responsibility on my shoulders. You know very well it's not my fault if I get here late. The bus is slow, there's usually a traffic jam... And almost everybody who works here arrives late. Why do I always get the blame when the others are just as much at fault? It's not fair, you always single me out. Before you started working here, no one ever complained about my being late..."

And so on - mutual blame, accusation, protestations of innocence, suggestions of INJUSTICE in the world, etc. Complainers aren't the most difficult of difficult people. They don't provoke the mental confusion characteristic to the vitriolic attacks of aggressive types. What they say doesn't hurt as much as the cutting remarks of a surgical type.

But even the kindest and most gentle people end up not being able to stand them.

Never satisfied...

Complainers and other negative types are never satisfied. If you admire the way they look, they'll say something like, "Ha! What you don't know is that my blood pressure's high enough to explode any moment. What can I do? My daughter (or son) is giving me such headaches... My hair's going to turn white before I reach fifty..." and so on, in a flood of recrimination that's impossible to stop.

Defeatists...

You probably know some people who always respond to a suggestion by saying, "Oh, but it'll never work, I'm sure it won't..." and who consider their existence an interminable source of problems.

For this type of person, everything unpleasant that happens is caused by the malevolence or incompetence of others. For them, making an effort, being ingenious and competent, are not elements of success. Only luck can produce a favourable situation, and even then they may not be fortunate enough to regard it as such.

Pessimists...

These people find comfort in being pessimistic, and use it as a crutch, to attract other people's attention. Therefore, if you manage to help a complainer or other negative type get rid of his/her problem, s/he won't be grateful in the least, since what you've done, in reality, is take away one of their reasons for living! And the first thing they'll do is look for another reason, i.e. something else to complain about!

Complainers and other negative types, just like specialists of the cutting remark, are expert at spreading the poison in their minds without letting anyone know about it.

Example:

Listen to this short conversation, which might give you a feeling of "deja-vu."

"Cash number 2 didn't total up right yesterday, Madeline. I was wondering if..."

"If you knew how careful I am when I do my totals, you wouldn't come complaining to me about it. And if you didn't let more than one person handle a cash, you wouldn't have these kinds of problems. We don't even have a system for knowing who used which cash, and when..."

"I know Madeline. The accountant has to get a better system in place soon."

"A better system? We don't even have a system! Listen, it's not my job to worry about things like this, but since you're accusing me..."

You do understand, don't you? Madeline, using great skill, deflected the blame back to her superior. She was able to put him on the defensive, and avoid the subject of her own possible errors.

Although this attitude is not ideal for getting promoted (since bosses don't like to admit they're at fault) Madeline did manage to avoid assuming any responsibility for the situation.

Forever victims...

Madeline falls into the "difficult person" category, since she always places herself in the role of victim. Even though she's completely in the right, and in no way responsible for the cash error, she is nevertheless a source of embarrassment to her boss since he "can't tell her anything" without provoking a similar scene - the most insignificant criticism is enough to send her sulking off like a beaten dog, or wailing to the washroom.

A destructive influence

It's obvious that complainers and other negative types exercise a destructive influence on the people around them, often without being aware of it themselves. Their presence in a working group can be catastrophic.

Skeptical? Well, read a little further.

Example:

Listen to a young natural science professor, recently hired by a private junior college:

"At the present time we only have one microscope for every six students. That gives you some idea of how poor we are in equipment. How am I supposed to give a course in histology or pathology without a microscope for every two, or at worst three students? Obviously we lack money. But every time I bring the matter up with the headmaster, I come out of his office feeling depressed for the rest of the week. He has a stock response to whatever suggestions I make for raising funds: "No one would agree, it'll never work. The personnel would never go along with the idea. We tried it a few years ago, without success." Of course, he knows his job and may be he's right..."

As you see, a negative attitude can easily become contagious and undermine the whole team's morale. That's the most dangerous thing about it.

Nevertheless, although they do fall into the category of "difficult" people by draining our enthusiasm, our energy and zest for life, negative persons don't deserve the same drastic treatment as we would accord a surgical aggressive type.

They may be sensitive...

Often these people act in good faith, and do not harbour any harmful intentions. So nothing positive will be achieved by verbally abusing them.

Make an effort, both for yourself and for them. You'll feel proud and pleased to have been able to help them - and help yourself at the same time.

How to help others and yourself at the same time

The best solution is to somehow open the door to the prison of passivity and futility that such people live in - and try to get you to live in as well - by refusing to get sucked in to the cycle of "accusation - defence - accusation."

If you can't do this, then the only remaining course of action is for you to protect yourself against their influence by remaining indifferent, or by getting away as soon as possible.

Let's start at the beginning. Here's a strategy you can use:

1. Find out exactly what the grievances are

To do this you first have to listen attentively, as difficult as that may seem. Because it's likely that if you have a complainer in your midst, no one has really listened to him/her for a long time, since all s/he does is gripe.

Let the person know that you're interested, and that you understand what s/he's talking about. In other words, show that you are receptive to his/her problems.

For example:

Let's say your brother-in-law is always complaining about his wife's (your sister's) behaviour:

"And then she tells me it's my fault the children are always tired these days. She says it's because we can't take a vacation. But I have too much to do at work, I'm putting in a lot of overtime, and my hours aren't steady. Not like her... her job is a lot less demanding than mine. I do what I can, but you understand how hard it is, with the new boss... etc."

Here's how you can proceed:

This conversation is more like a self-hypnotic speech that the brother-in-law has been carrying on with himself for a long time. You have to interrupt the flow by doing something unusual - raise your hand and say something like:

"Just hold on a minute. I want to understand exactly what the problem is. My sister says the kids are tired because you didn't go on vacation. You say you can't go because you have too much work to do, and on top of that you have a new boss to deal with. Is that about right?"

Be careful! At this point, two kinds of traps may be laid for you, which you absolutely must avoid falling into:

Understanding doesn't mean you're in agreement

1. Letting someone know you understand what they're saying doesn't mean you agree with them. Far from it. If it did, you'd never be able to resolve the issue, since you'd be implying that you think the plaintiff is right and that you - or a third person who is the object of the complaint - are to blame. This will probably lead to a new series of grievances.

So avoid saying things like, "You're right..." or "I agree..." etc. which may be the easiest way to put an end to the discussion, but which doesn't solve anything.

At all costs, avoid the "persecutor - victim - saviour" triangle

At all costs, avoid the "persecutor - victim - saviour" triangle. When someone complains, s/he automatically assumes the role of victim: "They did this to me... they're out to get me... they don't care about me... etc." The person's moaning and groaning always seems to have an exterior cause.

Wherever there's a victim, there's a persecutor - someone who persecutes the victim. And although the victim may not come right out and say it, you are placed in the role of persecutor.

"The children are upset and hard to control these days because they don't see enough of you, and because they know we're not going on vacation..."

"But honey, you know very well that I can't just stop working..." and off you go, trying to justify yourself, which is an implicit confession of your guilt. The complainer has now succeeded: you are the bad one, and you have to exonerate yourself by paying more attention to your spouse (which is really what the whole argument is about!).

This type of exchange leads directly to a cycle of "accusation - defence - accusation" which goes nowhere except to make you feel like a victim in turn, and start a new round of bickering with your own accusations.

And it can get get worse, if a third person enters the ring. Because whenever you have a victim and a persecutor, a golden opportunity arises for someone to play the role of saviour! When you lend a sympathetic or compassionate ear to the complaints of a negative type, you're setting yourself up in the role of saviour.

In the preceding example, we saw how your brother-in-law came to you and told you about his problems with your sister. You may be tempted to reply by saying something like:

"Of course, old buddy, I understand and I'm going to talk to her about it." And there you are, committed to a role which you will surely regret having assumed later on. Because in a "victim - saviour - persecutor" triangle, the roles often get changed around.

If you speak to your sister in the role of her husband's saviour, you may soon become a victim yourself, since she could very well tell you to mind your own business. Or you may be cast in the role of persecutor - she will accuse you of trying to assassinate her by siding with her husband. Or you may end up completely confused and not knowing who to save, after your sister pours out all her troubles - trying to carry the load of a working woman and a mother while her husband spends all his time socialising in the guise of making contacts at work, etc.

There aren't many of us who haven't fallen into this kind of trap. But for your own good, and for the good of the people you're trying to help as well, it is essential to make every effort to avoid this kind of pitfall.

2. Suggest other concrete options

Once you've accurately summarised the situation, analyse each grievance and suggest other possible courses of action to the complainer other than his/her usual impotent reaction.

But be careful!

You'll have to demonstrate your creativity and suggest a number of alternatives. The complainer must then make a decision. It's not for you to decide what the complainer should or should not do. Don't try to impose your will. All you want to do is offer more choices. After that, it's essential that the person decide for him/herself.

Also, if you really want to help the person break out of the infernal cycle of complaining, then make your suggestions realistic.

To do this, you may have to find out more about the situation. Reformulate, in your own words, what you've understood so far, and ask a few specific questions.

Let's look at our example...

"And then she tells me it's my fault the children are always tired these days. She says it's because we can't take a vacation. But I have too much to do at work, I'm putting in a lot of overtime, and my hours aren't steady, like hers. Her job is a lot less demanding than mine. I do what I can, but you understand how hard it is, with the new boss... etc."

First show that you understand the problem:

"Wait a minute, I want to understand what's going wrong. My sister says the kids are tired because you didn't go on vacation. You feel you can't leave work because you have so much to do, and because you have a new boss to deal with. Is that about right?"

Don't allow any more complaining. If you are familiar with the situation, get right to the solutions.

"Okay, you have a number of choices:

- 1. You stay at home, and your wife and kids go on vacation.
- 2. You decide that your family's happiness is more important than pleasing your new boss.
- 3. You don't think your kids need a vacation after a hard school year, so you refuse your wife's request and make a great impression with the new boss."

At this point you can suggest a more methodical technique that will force the person to make a choice:

"What you can do to make deciding easier is to take a sheet of paper and write down the advantages and disadvantages of each option. Then you compare them, and make the right decision."

3. Help people become aware of their responsibility

Let's look at the motives behind the complaints made by Joanne, a forty year old woman who suddenly found herself alone after getting divorced. She lived through a period of deep emotional shock when she found out her husband was having an affair with a woman ten years her junior, whom he'd met at work. The divorce happened very quickly, totally upsetting her life, and she hasn't been able to regain her sense of equilibrium since.

Three years later Joanne is well established in her role of complainer. She confronts life as if she were the innocent victim of a terrible drama. She feels lonely and abandoned. Her old friends and acquaintances don't want to see her, fed up as they are with hearing the same old stories about how she was mistreated:

"I was always a good wife! I never said anything when he came home late, never asked for explanations... He didn't want to have children, so we didn't have any. He liked to go to the mountains, I liked the seaside - so we went to the mountains! All that so he could abandon me like a rusty old car and run off with a younger woman!"

Of course, playing this tired song over and over again obviously did nothing to help Joanne find a new companion. Then comes the day when she runs into you, or me...

When we show an interest in finding out more about her, she winds up the old phonograph and tells her story: "I was always a good wife... etc." And we get the whole spiel.

We can leave it at that, or we can recount our own tragedy (misery loves company), or we can prudently maintain our distance. But what if we want to help her? Here's how to proceed:

Ask a question

"Joanne, would you like to solve this problem?"

The answer will certainly be yes, since complainers are suffering and want to stop, at least outwardly. They feel trapped because they don't know what to do.

Of course if Joanne says, "No, leave me alone with my suffering!" then it would be useless to continue.

But say she agrees - yes, she wants to solve the problem. You have the time to spare - there's no reason not to try.

"If you want to put an end to this, you'll have to answer my questions with complete honesty. All right? Ready? Here's the first question: How do you blame yourself for your husband's leaving you?"

Joanne is speechless. She's just explained how she's the innocent victim in the whole affair, and here you are asking her to take the responsibility! She looks around nervously, playing for time. She did promise to answer honestly... Finally she says, "Really, I didn't want him to leave me!"

You continue: *"All right, you didn't want it, but in some ways you may have encouraged it to happen... put a little oil on the fire when things were going badly, perhaps?"*

Joanne is able to think more calmly and replies: "Well I wasn't going to welcome him back with open arms when I found out he was cheating on me. I made a terrible scene. I cried and shouted at him, made him realise all the things I'd done for him, all the sacrifices I'd made..."

"And you don't think that had something to do with his leaving?"

Joanne is pensive. She reviews the events of her divorce in her mind. She starts to see how she might have been at least partly to blame for the separation. But she can't accept it yet.

Now you can say something like: "All right, according to you, the way you reacted to your husband's infidelity was not the main reason he left. But why did you let him leave, if you wanted so much to keep him?"

Watch Joanne's face - you'll see the curse that's been haunting her and condemning her to a life of solitude lift away, like a veil being removed. Her face lights up... "You're right! I was happy when he left, the bastard..."

And your work is done.

Don't say anything more just yet.

Leave Joanne (or a person like her) alone with her thoughts for a few moments. The way she remembers a whole section of her life has to be re-arranged. She is starting to see the separation in a new light, from a different perspective, where she no longer has to play the role of victim.

The danger here is if she says... "Yes BUT..." and goes on to come up with new rationalisations for playing her old sad song. But with a little skill on your part, you can help the person invent a new version of events, where her role is more positive and attractive. This is what she has to do to liberate herself, and you've given her the opportunity to do so!

Set aside everything that isn't your responsibility

If things go well with Joanne, we can ask the following question: "You say you felt happy that he left... Now try to remember what you might have done to provoke his leaving, to encourage it or permit it... For now, just set aside everything that isn't your responsibility, and tell me about the separation as if it were your doing, instead of you being an unwilling victim..."

If Joanne is able to do this, it means she's completely liberated. It may be difficult for her, or seem like an artificial exercise, since she was so strongly attached to the old version of events.

But for her own good, insist that she continue. Get her to tell you the story the way you want to hear it. And stop her at the slightest tendency to relapse into a complaining mode, and correct her immediately.

In this way, Joanne will rebuild her self image and become a person capable of causing changes in her relationship with a man. And although she may have been responsible for a negative change in the past, she can also initiate positive changes in the present, which is far from the worst thing a person can be, which is to be powerless.

Another way to make someone assume responsibility

There are many ways we can conceive of our place in the universe. One consists of seeing ourselves as a minuscule and insignificant point in a vast and powerful universe, like a piece of straw being blown around by the immense forces of nature, with no control of any kind. This is what is called a "deterministic" concept.

According to this philosophy I can do nothing to change what happens to me, whether it's good or bad. I'm a prisoner in the flow of history, crushed by crises in the economy, or threatened by the increase in urban violence, or worn down with age, crowded out by the new generation... What can I do? Nothing!

"I'm late because: the weather was so bad; there was a traffic jam; my wife forgot to fill the tank after she used the car; there's a public transit strike; I live too far from work; a cop stopped me on the highway; there was a demonstration that blocked traffic; a truck double parked in the middle of the road; I had a flat tire... etc."

You may have noticed that people who are chronically late have an amazing imagination, and come up with astonishingly creative ways to explain why it wasn't their fault. And it's never their fault. They are the innocent victims of climactic, social or mechanical forces which are beyond their control.

This is how they keep a clean conscience. But the price you pay for hiding behind these kinds of arguments is much higher than they imagine. Because what they're admitting is that they have no power over themselves, or over the environment in which they live. If they don't even have the power to arrive on time, then obviously they don't have the power to do anything that could improve their existence.

Obeying unconscious prohibitions means being condemned to impotence

One of the ways human beings condemn themselves to a life of impotence is to abandon the power of being themselves, and obeying all kinds of commands which act in a hypnotic way, and which they are not aware of. These commands are often prohibitions, which have been planted in their brains at a very early age, and have been completely forgotten by their conscious minds. Nevertheless, these commands continue to exert a powerful and constant influence on their behaviour.

"Be perfect! Be nice! Be polite! Be strong (men don't cry...) Be fast! Work hard!"

A sign that someone is under the influence of such hypnotic commands is the habit of starting sentences with, "I should..." or "I have to..."

You'll notice these phrases a lot in the way complainers and other negative types express themselves:

"I have to get up every morning and I have to go to work. I have to put up with my clients' moods and, what's more, I have to put on a happy face. What hell!"

To really help a negative person, you have to get him or her to adopt a different understanding of his place in the universe. The minuscule and insignificant point must become aware that it has some weight, that it's capable of standing on its own two feet, despite the laws of gravity, and the fact that asserting oneself will have certain consequences. This attitude is called "creativism."

It is true that we are surrounded by forces that are beyond our control. But it's also true that there are things around us which are the undeniable demonstration of the immense power we exercise on ourselves and on our environment.

Lift your gaze from this page and you'll probably see walls that have been built by human hands. Whatever materials they're made of, you can be sure that a relatively short time ago, they didn't exist. People just like you planned them and built them. They are an undeniable demonstration of creative energy. No one was under an irrefutable obligation to build them. And you can modify this creation if you wish, by changing its colour or putting up a painting. Or you can destroy it if you like, wipe it right off the face of the earth like a sand castle. Because destroying is also an exercise of creative power.

You have the choice of seeing yourself as powerful and responsible, or impotent and irresponsible. To help negative persons achieve liberation, you first have to get them to assume responsibility for what they do, and for the consequences resulting from their actions.

To do this, use the following method.

Example

Complainer: "I have to get up every morning and I have to go to work..."

You: *What would happen if you didn't get up one day?"*

Complainer: "My boss would give me hell."

You: *"And if you didn't go to work for a few days, what would happen then?"*

Complainer: "I'd get fired."

You: *"And if you lost your job, then what would happen?"*

Complainer: "Well, with the economic situation being what it is, I'd have a lot of trouble finding another job..."

You: *"And if you weren't able to find a job, what would happen?"*

Complainer: "I'd live in poverty. My wife would probably leave me. They'd cut off the electricity... the phone... I'd have to move out of my apartment... and I'd end up living on the street like a bum."

You: *"And what would happen if you lived like a bum?"*

Complainer: *"Well, I'd be very unhappy."*

You: *"So if I understand correctly, if you decided not to get up in the morning you'd become a bum and you'd be very unhappy?"*

Complainer: *"Right."*

"So you prefer getting up in the morning to being a bum?"

"Yes."

"Then you get up in the morning because you CHOOSE to!"

Now the tables are turned. If a person chooses to do something instead of feeling obliged to do it, s/he becomes the master of his destiny, and can no longer play the role of victim.

I have to:	A
If I don't do (A) then	B
And if (B) then	C
And if (C) then	D
And if (D) then	

... and so on until option Z.

I prefer A to Z...

THEREFORE I CHOOSE "A"

You can expect seasoned complainers to keep arguing that they are "still obliged to..." even after you make them realise that in reality they choose to do what they do in order to avoid unpleasant consequences, or to obtain substantial benefits.

Don't be taken in by these arguments, whatever they are. Ask the question:

"Is there anyone pointing a gun to your head? Is anyone threatening to kill you if you don't obey? And even if there were, wouldn't you prefer to die rather than do something you find unacceptable?"

Examples of persons choosing this extreme option are numerous, which demonstrates that we can remain in control of our destiny and be responsible for our choices, no matter what situation we find ourselves in.

4. Last resort: get them mad!

If, in your charitable efforts to help a negative person, all the methods suggested above fail, then you're dealing with someone whose resigned attitude is deeply ingrained. S/he has been living for so long with a sense of impotence that s/he identifies almost completely with it.

You can decide not to see such persons again, or see them as seldom as possible in order to protect yourself against their negative influence. You know that defeatism is contagious, and you have every right to take care of yourself by breaking off relations with chronically difficult people. You don't owe them anything, just because they happen to be poor victims and you're all right. Don't forget the terrible psychological trap - persecutor / victim / saviour - described earlier in this chapter.

However, you may not be in a position to avoid the person if, say, they are a close relative or a colleague at the office. Or it may just be someone you absolutely refuse to abandon.

There's still hope for them - a final assault is still possible. Don't forget that there are hidden resources in all human beings, even when the hazards of life have buried them so deeply they seem irretrievable.

As we've seen, complainers and other negative types are "low energy" people. They walk around as if they were carrying a hundred pound weight on their shoulders.

Don't expect a hardened negative personality to suddenly become highly motivated about something. That would be asking too much. What are they supposed to do - forget all of a sudden about the gross injustices and tragedies they've had to bear up to now?

Getting angry is in itself a sign of progress for these people. It means getting them to shake off the weight that is crushing them, and making them rebel against what they believe is their destiny. They'll experience a surge of energy - misdirected of course - but much better than the listless passive existence they've been trapped in for so long.

Provoke them so that their anger is directed at you. This can be done by challenging what they say, and the way they say it. Don't let them get away with using words and phrases that enhance their image of impotent victim. You have to systematically insist that they specify exactly what they mean, and get them to alter their perception of events so that they finally assume responsibility for their own lives.

This technique is used with great skill and scientific precision by psychologists to help difficult persons overcome their negativity. In your case, although you may not be a psychologist, you do know how to ask questions.

The worst that can happen, if you're not skillful enough, is that the person gets mad at you. And as we've already said, even that would constitute some progress!

Example:

Let's listen to what John has to complain about:

"It's always the same old story. Every time we visit her parents, we have to sit there and listen to them put us down. I know I shouldn't say it, but everyone knows it isn't my fault. I'm discouraged, and I get the feeling nobody gives a damn about me..."

Here's what you're going to do. As you listen to John talking, interrupt him every time he says something that isn't completely exact. John: "It's always the same old story..." You: "Always? Really always? Hasn't there been just one time

when it was different?" Of course there has. Nothing is always the same, and the only permanent thing in the entire universe is change. So you insist that John reformulate the statement by saying: "Very often..." or "Nine times out of ten..." instead of always.

Get the person to concentrate on the positive side

Now you've established the possibility of saying something like, "And what about the time it wasn't the same... what happened then?" By so doing you force the person to concentrate on the positive aspects of the situation.

John: "Every time..."

You: "Every time? Really? Hasn't there been even one time when...? (Same procedure as for the word "always").

John: "... that we go and visit..."

You: "We? Who's we?"

Make the person say "I" - get them to repeat the sentence using the first person. This is already an important step towards assuming responsibility for their actions.

John: "I have to sit there and put up with..."

You: "You have to? Who says you have to? What would happen if you didn't just sit there? What would the worst case scenario be if you didn't? (And you continue with the method "I have to... I choose to..." described earlier.)

John: "I know I shouldn't..."

You: "Who said you shouldn't? What would happen if you did?" (Same procedure as before.)

John: "But everybody knows that..."

You: "Everybody? But who exactly? Because I personally know of examples that are different."

At this point the person, if s/he hasn't already exploded, will say something like... "Who exactly? I don't know... ME! That's who!"

Now you can ask: "You? Well how do you know?" This forces the person to come up with concrete facts.

John: "It isn't..."

You: "What do you mean by "it"?

The person has to explain what "it" means. Does "it" refer to the bad relationship with the parents? Or does "it" stand for his own impotence to influence the situation, to be accepted by them? In other words, the word "it" creates an unclear, grey area which the person must clarify.

John: "I'm discouraged..."

You: "Discouraged by what? By whom?" (Once again, insist on concrete facts.)

John: "I get the feeling nobody gives a damn about me..."

You: "Nobody? Really nobody? Isn't there anybody in the whole world who appreciates you just a little?" Honesty will force the person to admit that you, at least, must like him since you're giving him so much of your precious time and attention! He will have to reformulate the sentence and say something like, "I get the feeling a lot of people don't like me..." Even then, you should force him to reveal who exactly he thinks doesn't like him.

A very powerful method

As you can see, this method of asking questions is powerful. A complainer who is challenged in this way will either end up fighting back, or refuse to see you any more.

But take care! Don't use the method on people you don't know very well, or whom you're dependent on, like a superior at work or a supplier.

Imagine what would happen if your boss said something like, "I always have to make concessions with them..." and you reply, "Well first of all, sir, what do you mean by saying you have to?

And does it really always happen, or are there exceptions? And who exactly do you mean by "them"?

The results of your questioning may not be entirely to your advantage in this situation!

What to do if you feel your efforts have failed?

Before deciding that your initiative to help someone has been a failure, persevere even if you get the feeling you're banging your head against a wall. Don't become a defeatist too!

You'll have to deal with the other person's frustration. If s/he's been a complainer for a long time, then you mustn't expect your rational suggestions to have an immediate effect. You may even provoke a whole new series of complaints, in which case you may get irritated and start to lose interest.

Don't give up now! Take a few deep breaths, then interrupt the stream of complaints and start again. Sometimes just saying something like: "All right, but let's get back to the question I asked earlier on..." may be enough to do the trick.

Because you see, with chronic complainers, just like with surgical aggressive types (although for different reasons) it's futile to try to be tactful or polite. These people are too obsessed by their problems to get upset if you interrupt them or insist they be more specific.

So don't hesitate to interrupt by raising your voice or using a gesture to get them to stop talking.

Your training programme

Dealing with complainers and other negative types, listening to them, helping them put an end to their lamentations and getting them to take positive measures, requires an unusual degree of objectivity and neutrality. After all, life throws so many problems our way, we don't have to make them the main subject of our conversation!

Nevertheless, if you wish to assert yourself, both with others and with yourself, you have to learn to resolve this kind of problem. Your career may be at stake, or an important relationship, or simply your peace of mind. So make the necessary effort - the rewards are well worth it.

Transform your own history as a "victim"

Who can claim they've never suffered from injustice or been badly treated by others? We're all victims at some time or other, either during childhood or as adults. We probably don't think much about these incidents, which is why we don't fall into the category of complainer.

However, if you want to help others by using the "re-writing history" technique, you first have to be able to use it on yourself.

So take a sheet of paper and note the circumstances where you felt like a victim.

When your list is complete, answer these three questions:

- How did my behaviour contribute to making this happen?
- What did I do to encourage the situation? (Give precise facts)
- How did I let this happen?

If you found a number of incidents where you felt like a victim, do the exercise for each one. You'll feel lighter, as if a burden has been lifted from your mind, and you'll experience a renewed sense of your own power.

Root out your false obligations

Now write a list of fifty things (at least) that you feel obligated to do, starting each sentence with "I HAVE TO..."

- "I have to declare my income..."
- "I have to visit my wife's parents..."
- "I have to water the lawn..." etc.

Start here:

When the list is complete, read it over and take the time to become aware of how you feel about it all.

Write down how you feel.

Now take your fifty obligations and write them down again, only this time use the words "I CHOOSE TO..." at the beginning of each sentence.

- "I choose to declare my income..."
- "I choose to visit my wife's parents..."
- "I choose to mow the lawn..."

Finished? Now how do you feel? Take a moment to add any other positive things you do that come to mind, using "I choose to..." to start the sentence.

If you take the time to apply the "I have to - I choose to" process, described earlier, for each obligation, you may find that the worst possible consequence of not doing action "A" is still preferable to doing action "A". In this case, you will know that you can choose not to do "A".

For example, you can choose not to water the lawn, in which case the grass will dry up and you won't have a lawn anymore. If you don't care, then that's fine (and you'll also be saving water, money on fertiliser, etc.)

This exercise may help you discover something about your real power over the world around you, and make you a freer person. Then you can go on to share the experience with the complainers you meet and help them, in turn, assume responsibility for their choices. Keep a journal

As you saw in the previous chapter, it can be very useful to keep a journal of your encounters with difficult people, both complainers and other negative types.

Use the following model:

Place and date:
Situation:
First round:
1- What the other person said:
2- How I replied:
3- How I SHOULD HAVE REPLIED:
Second round:
1- What the other person said:
2- How I replied:
3- How I SHOULD HAVE REPLIED:

CHAPTER 4
Clams

What are clams like?

Portrait No. 1

Noticing that his new neighbour was working in the garden, Jack remembered something he wanted to ask him. So he walked over to the hedge, a smile on his face, said hello and tried to start a discussion.

"Your daughter and mine are in the same class..."

No reaction.

"And Helen told me she likes Claire a lot. Did Claire say anything to you?"

The neighbour responds with an indistinct grunt.

"I thought that, since the girls are becoming such good friends, we could work out some kind of arrangement for babysitting, if it's convenient of course. That way we both wouldn't have to call someone in..."

"Hm..."

The neighbour continues working on his lettuce in silence.

"Well, if it doesn't work for you, we'll have to figure out something else..." Jack sighs and walks away.

Portrait No. 2

An economist has to present a verbal summary of a report she prepared for her superior, which he was supposed to have read beforehand. She states her conclusions, and then waits for her boss to comment:

"Mmm..."

"Is there something you don't understand? Maybe I should clarify some of the points..."

" Mm, no..."

"Well what do you think? Is it all right? Can we send it to the printer as is?"

"Well... hm..."

"Sir! Will you just tell me what you think and get it over with!"

The economist ends up seeing red. Who can blame her? If she's in any way fatigued or under stress, she may even lose her temper and explode, which is often the kind of frustrated reaction clams provoke. And then there will be all kinds of repercussions to deal with.

If you're confronted with a clam, you'll be lucky to get a response that's more than two syllables long! Clams are probably the most exasperating of difficult types. They close themselves off just when you're expecting a clear, precise response, or when you need an explanation, or when you're hoping to start a conversation, etc.

How can you differentiate between a clam and someone who just doesn't talk much?

You have to be careful. Laconic people are not necessarily clams. Some people only speak when they have something interesting to say. They're incapable of small talk. Other people will register what you say and then wait until they've come up with a coherent answer before replying.

So what is the difference between clams and people who just don't talk much? No doubt you'd like to know the answer to this question.

Well, whoever has had to deal with these two types will tell you that it's almost impossible to mix them up. Let's look at the two examples above, and imagine that Jack's neighbour and the economist's boss aren't really clams, but just persons who don't talk much.

Portrait No. 1

"Your daughter and mine are in the same class..."

No discernible reaction. The neighbour waits for what follows.

"And Helen told me she likes Claire a lot. Did Claire say anything to you?"

"Yes, she told me" (Or: "No, she didn't say anything to me about it..." It doesn't matter which).

"I thought that, since the girls are becoming such good friends, we could work out some kind of arrangement for babysitting, if it's convenient of course. That way both of us wouldn't have to call someone in..."

"I'll talk to my wife about it, if you like."

The neighbour goes back to weeding his lettuce. Although far from talkative, he's given Jack an adequate reply.

Portrait No. 2

An economist has to present a verbal summary of a report she prepared for her superior, which he was supposed to have read beforehand. She states her conclusions, and then waits for her boss to comment:

"Mmm..."

"Is there something you don't understand? Maybe I should clarify some of the points..."

"No, it all seems quite clear."

"Well what do you think? Can we send it to the printer as is?"

"Yes, go ahead." (Or: "No, let me think about it..." or "You should place more emphasis on such and such an aspect..." etc.)

Do you see the difference? Laconic persons don't beat around the bush when asked to respond to a direct or indirect question. They simply keep quiet when they have nothing further to say.

What can we deduce from a clam's behaviour?

The reasons why a person is unable to say anything while you're trying to communicate with him/her are much more varied than for the other difficult types we've looked at up to now.

There are a number of kinds of clams, all very different from each other, which should make you be very careful when interpreting their behaviour. In fact, the only way to get an accurate idea of what's going on is to make the clam talk, and to listen very closely to what s/he says.

The silence of rejection or punishment

Becoming an inexpressive wall of silence to express resentment is a weapon you may have used yourself. Or you may have been its victim. I was once the target of this type of behaviour, and I must say it was one of the hardest situations to deal with in my relations with difficult people.

There are people whose resentment is so strong they remain stubbornly silent for extremely long periods, and resist all attempts at opening up to communication. Couples who have stopped talking to each other for seemingly innocuous reasons, and who only communicate through written notes, have been humorously portrayed in films and books. However, when it happens in real life - when parents stop talking to their children or to each other - the situation, far from being funny, is serious, and can become dangerous.

You can understand a person being silent after a fight. But how can you explain it when it occurs with someone you've had absolutely no cause to disagree with?

First of all, you may fall into a category which the clam rejects systematically. We all know about the kinds of twisted thinking that turns some people into racist, religious or ideological fanatics.

The simple fact of having differently shaped eyes, or talking with an accent, or just being perceived as an outsider or someone who is better off, can be enough to trigger the clam reaction.

This is the same as an adolescent who refuses to communicate with an adult because s/he mistrusts ALL adults.

And this is the worst kind of rejection to accept, because it's so difficult to understand. Unless you have some inside information about the person who is rejecting you in this way, you'll probably ask yourself, "What is it about me that this person cannot accept?" or "What have I done to him/her?"

Don't expect these clam types to explain their motives and feelings to you. Doing so would imply recognising you as a separate and equal human being, which is exactly what they refuse to do. And they would also be forced to justify their irrational and iniquitous feelings, which they don't even admit they have!

The irrational and extremist aspects of this kind of rejection may lead you to think that there's nothing you can do about it. However, that is not the case.

Automatic rejection mechanism

A person who behaves in this way reduces you to one or two characteristics which serve to justify the rejection, and remains blind to everything else about you, especially your qualities. As long as the person can maintain this image of you as a limited caricature, s/he can continue to cut off all attempts at communication by "clamming up."

This is due to the person's automatic rejection mechanism, which s/he can do nothing to control.

If you're dealing with someone whom you don't know, and whom you probably won't see again, then there's really not much you can do to rectify the situation, unless you have some kind of magic power (like the ability to pull a little fluffy white rabbit out of a hat - who could resist that!).

But if you're going to be seeing the person on a regular basis, then you may have to do something about it. Fortunately, there's hope.

Above all stay calm, and if possible maintain a benevolent attitude toward the person. To change the basis of the relationship, you have to give the person a chance to know you better, and discover the multiple dimensions of who you are.

As soon as the clam starts to become aware of your other characteristics, it will be impossible to continue treating you in such a one dimensional fashion - you will be perceived in a new light.

The clam's precautionary attitude will melt like snow in the spring sunshine. It's highly probable that s/he will completely forget about the initial rejection you had to deal with, and start behaving normally towards you.

It's due to this phenomenon that groups of human beings are capable of being deadly enemies under one set of conditions, and then go on to live peacefully side by side under other conditions. Whenever hate rules the day, you can be sure to find mutual ignorance and a deformed view of reality as the underlying cause. But when the same communities live peacefully together, it's because they understand and appreciate each other. This is both a result of their proximity, and also a basic condition of their peaceful co-existence.

The silence of protection or avoiding responsibility

"Madeline, can you tell me who screwed up the photocopy machine again? Whoever it was tried to make copies on acetate paper, and didn't use the right materials."

"Uuh..." (followed by embarrassed silence).

"I won't let it go this time! You're not leaving here until you tell me who is responsible..."

Madeline's face turns to stone. No one is going to make her denounce her best friend. She resumes her work, ignoring the issue, and at the same time making it clear that she's not going to change her mind. Not knowing how to deal with the situation, her superior is forced to accept defeat.

Avoiding painful confrontation

When someone clams up in order to avoid conversation, it may be due to the fact that the person has something to hide and wishes, at all cost, to avoid a potentially painful confrontation.

Refusing to answer a question, or answering in indistinct monosyllables, allows a person to avoid having to lie, and it's unlikely you'll be able to get that person to change his / her mind.

The problem is simply that these people don't know how to lie. If Madeline had been able to smile sweetly and say, "I don't have the slightest idea who broke the machine..." then the only thing you could do would be to believe her, or call her an outright liar, which is a very serious accusation.

So you're dealing with someone who is prevented from lying by their own value system, and prevented from betraying a friend for the same reason. You can imagine the inner conflict this must be causing in Madeline!

She's paralysed. Her last resort is to remain silent, and avoid looking at you. But as we'll see later on in this chapter, even silence transmits a message, and you'll learn how to decipher these messages so that you can read clam types like an open book.

In Madeline's case, you would order her to look into your eyes, and then recite the names of the people who work in the office, or whom you know have access to the machine.

Madeline can still say nothing, but she certainly won't have enough control over her emotions to prevent her from making some sign when the culprit's name is mentioned - she'll blush, or turn away- and you'll know who it is.

Then all you have to do is confront the guilty party and prove you're right. If the person turns out to be another "difficult" case, you'll know exactly what to do.

The silence of emotional repression

Gilbert comes home and finds his wife upset. It isn't the first time, and he recognises the signs immediately. Worried, he asks, "Is anything wrong?" but this just irritates her more. "No!" she snaps back.

Of course this response solves nothing. Gilbert is sure something happened, but his wife just goes about her business getting supper ready, an absent look in her eyes, her movements a little jerky, like a robot.

Finally Gilbert loses patience. He has to know what happened. "Listen," he says, his voice tense, "something's bothering you. You're not yourself. Tell me what happened!"

"Nothing, nothing at all!"

And the more she refuses to talk, the more certain Gilbert is that something is really wrong.

Later on in the evening he asks her again, and she suddenly bursts out crying. "Monica has breast cancer!" Despite the bad news,

Gilbert feels a whole lot better. There's nothing worse than not knowing, than being kept in the dark, is there?

Monica is Gilbert's sister-in-law. His wife starts sobbing desperately. Gilbert tries to comfort her, without much success. However, the worst of the crisis will be over in a couple of minutes. Then she'll be able to tell him the story more calmly, after which she'll probably feel exhausted and need to sleep.

Gilbert did the right thing in helping her release her emotions.

Another man could have reacted very differently in a similar situation. He may have assumed that his wife's behaviour was due to some error she committed, and immediately blame her and get upset himself. He could have shut himself off like a clam as well, saying something like, "Well, since you refuse to come clean, it's none of my business!".

More often than we think, people suppress their emotional crises by hiding behind silence. They grit their teeth and refuse to let others know about their pain, knowing that if they let themselves go, even for a moment, they'll be swept away in a tide of emotion.

It's healthy to be able to express our emotions

If a suppressed emotion is not expressed somehow, it stagnates, and remains pent up somewhere in the body, where it does its nasty work tensing muscles, causing cramps, skin rashes, ulcers, etc. As time passes, all conscious recollection of the initial emotion may disappear. But the body never forgets. So it's much better to express pain or anger. The way you can help clam types is by giving them an opportunity to open up, instead of remaining blocked, teeth clenched, in stony silence, because they are afraid to cry.

So don't be surprised if your efforts to get a clam to talk results in the person bursting into tears. If you're not prepared, you may be somewhat frightened by the disproportionate intensity of the person's reaction.

Remember what you've just read. You are not the cause of the person's suffering. All you did was open a door, and all you have to do is remain quietly by the person's side, ready to offer your kind assistance. You don't have to do anything special - just pass the kleenex, and if the person is a friend, maybe offer some physical contact - a hug or a pat on the back.

Provoking such outpourings of emotion in the workplace would be embarrassing. However, you can't expect your colleagues to be completely free of emotion. Try to discern any hidden motives which may lie behind their refusal to communicate. Try to find out what the real problem is.

If you feel that the person is too charged up emotionally, stop! Suggest s/he see the company doctor, or take a few days off. Your role in the workplace is not to provide emotional therapy...

The silence of incomprehension and boredom

Haven't you ever been to some kind of social gathering where you know absolutely no one, have nothing in common with the persons present, and where your teeth remain locked tight for the entire evening because you can't find anything of value to say? This is the final, and most common motive behind the behaviour of the clam types you're likely to run across. These people live on another planet. They don't understand you, and don't know how to communicate with you. Because of this, they may find your company boring, but this isn't always the case.

This situation reminds me of a young woman, with whom I had a passionate affair. She was ravishingly beautiful, and we felt an immediate physical attraction. When we held hands, a powerful current of emotion flowed between us.

But aside from that, she was completely silent with me. None of the topics of conversation I brought up could get her to say one word. She listened to me, devouring me with her eyes, and whenever I stopped talking there was a dead silence. And this silence wasn't only between us - I knew it was the same with all her friends.

She was really in love with me, and proved it by crossing an entire continent just to be with me, while I was hoping she'd stay where I'd left her. Because just the idea of living through more of those painful silences gave me the shivers.

In my opinion, a relationship is not based solely on physical attraction, and with this woman I experienced the boredom of love. At the time, I had no idea why such an insurmountable barrier existed between us, despite our physical affinity. But my research in later years helped me find the answer.

Do you speak the same language?

You may think, as I once did, that all you have to do to communicate with someone is speak the same language. I speak English, you speak English, so we can communicate, right? Wrong.

Martine: "I'm listening to you, but I don't know what you're talking about. It really makes no sense to me."

Mark: "Can't you see what I'm doing! I'm trying to use a little imagination to get you to understand what I mean."

Violet: "I really don't feel you're making sense either. Your images just leaves me cold." Do you think these three people have a chance of of understanding each other? Maybe, but to do so they'll have to make a concerted effort to translate what they're saying. That's right, translate. Martine uses a predominantly auditory language, while Mark's language is visual, and all his expressions are of a visual kind. Violet, on the other hand, uses words that refer to her feelings only.

Three ways of perceiving the world

These three ways of perceiving the world are related to our three principle senses: hearing, sight and touch. How can these people use their senses so differently, since none of them are deaf, blind or unable to feel?

Contemporary psychologists have made in depth studies of of these behavioural differences, which also lie at the heart of our communication problems. They showed that an individual selects information perceived through the five senses.

Sometimes we're all ears, at other times we depend solely on our vision, at others we're extremely sensitive to touch. We can also be overwhelmed by the odour of perfume, or by the taste of a delicious meal.

You will notice, for example, that it is very difficult to be fully attentive to what is being said around you while concentrating on some delicious taste. It is impossible to be fully conscious of the perceptions of all five senses at the same time.

We are constantly selecting and concentrating on a single aspect of our experience.

This selection process begins at a very early age. Every one of us was conditioned to place more emphasis on what we heard, saw or felt. By the time we reach adulthood, we are firmly ensconced in one of three groups: "hearers", "see-ers" or "feelers."

Because of this we develop preferences for the plastic arts, for music, or for dance. Or we are affected by physical appearance, or the quality of a person's voice, or by touch. There are many more ways that people differ, simply because we don't use our five senses in the same way.

But is this sufficient to explain why some people shut themselves off from you? Possibly. Let's look at the case of my silent lover. We could communicate through touching in a fairly intense manner, which explains the attraction between us. But apart from that, we lived in two separate universes. She was a visual person, content with what her eyes perceived. I am an auditory type, and I place a lot of emphasis on the sound of someone's voice.

But that wasn't the only reason for her silence. There were other differences that made our reaching a common understanding highly improbable.

The principles of affinity

Having an affinity for someone means feeling close to that person naturally, without effort. "Instant sympathy" could be another term for it, although affinities don't always appear the first time you meet someone. You may have to get to know a person better before feeling a real affinity.

The opposite of affinity is the feeling of having nothing in common with a person, of having completely different interests. The result of such a relationship is boredom, indifference, and sometimes even hate. A lot of "clam" behaviour stems from this.

In addition to developing one sensory function more than the rest since childhood, we've also been equipped with filters that sort out the information we receive about the exterior world. Certain things attract our attention, others we ignore completely.

It's fortunate this process takes place, since our brains couldn't cope if we remained open to all incoming information, at all times, and with the same level of intensity. The disadvantage of this process is that we get only a partial and incomplete view of the world, and this leads to disagreements with persons whose perceptions are as fragmented as ours, but who have developed different sets of filters from our own.

That's why we tend to favour people who use the same filters as we do. When we perceive reality in the same way as someone else, we feel an immediate affinity for that person. When we don't use the same filters, we feel a gulf separating us, and we wonder what we can do to cross over.

Six ways of sorting information

Recent psychological studies have led to a clearer understanding of the multiple ways we construct our perception of reality.

Among all the ways we can differ from each other, one is of particular interest here.

To understand it better, think of the best vacation you can remember taking, or one that you would like to take. Depending on the category, or "tribe" you belong to, you may recall vividly coloured and varied images, or things you heard and said, or you'll remember it in terms of tactile sensations (heat, comfort, etc.) and emotions.

Set these aside, and what do you think of? Places? Activities? People? Events? Information? Certain objects?

These are the six main categories which you and I, and everyone else, use to sort information. This means that we're not interested in all dimensions of an event, and there are even some that we systematically ignore.

Dream vacations

Let's look at the example of our dream vacation. Say you find yourself in a travel agency, and the agent is trying to sell you a cruise to Greece.

The agent won't succeed by telling you about the marvellous LOCATIONS to be found in Greece if what you're interested in are the PEOPLE. Your decision will be based on whether your friend George is willing to accompany you, and on the kind of people you'll meet on the tour, and on whether or not the Greek natives have a reputation for being friendly to tourists.

Neither will the agent succeed by telling you that this cruise to Greece is a unique EVENT, since for the first time, the ship will be following the path traced by Ulysses centuries earlier, if what you're interested in is ACTION. If you're action oriented, you'll want to know about the activities available during the voyage. Diving? Windsurfing? Horseback riding and hiking?

As a last resort, the travel agent starts giving you all the information about the cruise - schedules, ports of call, distances you'll be travelling, exchange rates, average temperatures for that time of year, etc.

Pretty soon you stop listening - your mind is elsewhere, and you respond to the agent's questions in monosyllables. Because what you're interested in are THINGS. In fact, you walked into the travel agency in the first place because you were attracted by a magnificent Balinese mask in the window, and you wanted to know if it was for sale. Is there anything interesting to buy in Greece? That's what you want to know. An imitation amphora, or a woven carpet...

Talkative one day, silent another

With these examples in mind, you can begin to understand why people, you included, can stubbornly refuse to say a word, closing themselves off like a clam in its shell. A person may prattle on endlessly about his / her preferred activity, but have absolutely no interest in discussing office gossip, if his / her sorting criteria is ACTION rather than PEOPLE.

In the same way, it's not surprising that certain professions correspond to these different filters: to be a landscape architect, you have to prefer locations; a psychologist or teacher will prefer people; a researcher will concentrate on information; an antique dealer will be someone who is preoccupied with objects; a journalist with events; a sports professional with action.

No one filter is better or worse than another

It's important to remember that there are no value judgments being made about the different ways of perceiving reality that we've just mentioned. It's not "better" to be visual than auditory or tactile. There's no question of superiority or inferiority in being more attracted to action than people, or to objects rather than events.

The more we learn about human nature, the more we understand behaviour that may have seemed aberrant, and the more we can accept the differences between ourselves and others.

In fact, what you'd ideally want to do is discover which senses and which filters you use the least, and practice using them more. Doing so will develop your ability to perceive through all five senses, vastly increasing your sensitivity in all directions. And this will enable you to reach out to people who previously seemed inaccessible.

Because it is by speaking the same language, and adjusting your own point of view to suit their affinities, that you will be able to help people who have been locked in silence and incomprehension to open up and communicate. And the more you practice, the easier i t gets!

A few important recommendations for all clam types

First of all, stay calm. As we've seen, you may be tempted to interpret a person's silence as rejection, or give in to a desire to shake the person up in order to get some kind of reaction.

Don't!

There's nothing worse than saying or doing something that denigrates the other person. Don't think that a remark like:

"I get the feeling there's a sponge in your head instead of a brain!"

... will offend the person's pride and get him / her to suddenly start talking. On the contrary, this kind of remark will only fuel the clam's resolve to remain silent.

Let the person know that you're sincerely interested in listening, and you'll get what you want a lot more easily. This chapter has provided you with an understanding, and methods of dealing with a form of behaviour - silence - which can be caused by a wide variety of factors.

Now you have to study and practice the methods for overcoming this type of problem. (You'll soon be threatening people by saying, "I know how to make you talk...!")

At first, don't try to read between the lines. Get the person to talk. This avoids increased tension for yourself, and at the same time helps the other person.

1. Ask the right questions

You ask a colleague to join you in your office to discuss certain aspects of your work together. Unfortunately, you know that despite being very competent, this colleague has always been very closed with you in the past, perhaps because s/he lives in a world that's very different from your own.

However, you'd like to get the person to talk to you, because you're pretty sure s/he has some interesting ideas to offer.

To do this you can ask some questions. But not just any questions.

Avoid "closed" questions

As the name indicates, you're not going to get anywhere in your attempts to make someone open up to you by asking "closed" questions.

These are questions which can easily by answered by a simple "yes" or "no." For example, avoid questions like:

- "Do you have any comments?"
- "Could you give me your opinion?"
- "Can I count on you?"
- "Do you agree?"
- "Would you choose option A or B?"

These are dead end questions, and allow the clam to remain as shut off as ever.

Avoid insinuating questions

Some questions are really statements. Be careful you don't insinuate anything negative about the other person when asking a question.

For example, if you say, "Did you understand my question, or do I have to repeat it another ten times?"... you are insinuating that the other person isn't answering because s/he is an imbecile. As we've already seen, this is an excellent way not to get what you want.

On the other hand, making positive insinuations in the questions you ask is a good way to make a person comfortable.

For example, you could say jokingly:

"Do I understand from your silence that you do not wish to share your expertise with me?" Even in this slightly provocative way, you're still telling the person that you value his / her opinion.

Ask open-ended questions

As you can see, you have to ask questions that the clam, in all decency, cannot answer with a yes or a no only.

Let's look at our example. You could ask your colleague:

- "What do you think about this strategy?"

- "What suggestions do you have concerning this merger?" - "What is your opinion?"

- "Explain to me in detail how you see this being managed?" project

- "In your opinion, what are the advantages and disadvantages of this initiative?"

And so on...

Accompany your question with a sincerely inquisitive, but always polite glance, and maintain this expression after you've finished asking the question. Don't worry about the silence that may follow. Clams sometimes have trouble formulating their ideas rapidly, since they're not used to being called upon to do so. They may need a few moments to collect their thoughts.

Of course, hard core clam are able to avoid answering even the most open-ended questions. You aren't the first person who's tried to get them to open up!

Don't let silences embarrass you

Try to show that you aren't bothered at all by prolonged silences. Just let your expression do the talking, and wait patiently for a response. In our culture, a "prolonged silence" refers to a silence lasting ten seconds to two minutes, after which you have to say something to prevent both of you from falling asleep! Either that or your mind will start wandering.

Like other difficult types, clams have formed habits of ways to react to situations. This behaviour is in accord with their motive, which is to remain silent. They develop scenarios which they memorise - sometimes unconsciously - and which they use to get themselves off the hook without revealing anything.

That's why they're thrown off balance if you react in an unexpected way. They momentarily lose their apparent shell of assurance, which has enabled them to remain mute in the past, and you can use this breach in their defences to infiltrate their space by asking the right kind of questions.

Don't always try to fill the silences

There aren't many people who are comfortable when silences occur during a conversation or a meeting. This is one of the greatest handicaps western people have when negotiating with Asians. Japanese people can remain completely silent for ten minutes or more, their expression frozen into an inscrutable smile, while their American counterpart will desperately start looking for something to say after only a few seconds of silence. Under such circumstances, you can imagine how a lot of classified information is inadvertently revealed, which gives the Asian negotiators a clear advantage.

Clam types are constantly making use of this phenomenon. They know that every time they remain silent, someone else will volunteer to fill the gap.

Don't fall into this trap by getting upset, clearing your throat, sighing impatiently etc. And above all don't make small talk just to fill in the silent spaces.

So what should you do?

Repeat your open-ended question every twenty seconds, maintaining the same cordial, inquisitive expression, as many times as you have to.

If you think this is a little too militant, and feel guilty about forcing someone to speak out against their will, then ask yourself this question: is it better just to let a clam continue hiding? You know it isn't.

Well then, why not borrow a few harmless "spy" techniques, which have proven effective in the past? You interrogate the person, and then wait for an answer. If the person doesn't answer, you politely ask the same question again, and wait quietly until a response is forth coming.

Even the most hardened clam types will "crack" in the end.

They'll eventually understand that their game isn't going to work this time, that you're not reacting the way everybody else has in the past, and that they won't be able to manipulate you. You probably won't have to ask the question more than two or three times.

Try the "Suppose we..." technique

If you find the repeated interrogation technique too aggressive, there's another fantastic method for getting people to talk.

When you ask, "What is your opinion about this?" or "What do you think about such and such a subject?" the person may still remain silent, fearing that a response will implicate him /her in a discussion.

Providing a professional opinion, especially when you're not sure of yourself, can be compromising. Because even if you qualify your statements, you can be sure they'll be repeated as if you'd been certain of what you were saying.

Or you might refuse to answer a question like "What do you think we should do?" not because you don't know, but because you haven't had time to make up your mind. A tentative answer could be taken for a firm decision.

In the face of such reservations, the "Suppose we..." formula works wonders by removing the mental obstacle of making a commitment (even though the statement may be just as compromising as ever!).

Example 1:

"Gerry, where do you think you're going to spend you r vacation?"

(Gerry remains silent, meaning either "I don't know..." or "I haven't decided yet...")

"Suppose you already decided... where would it be?"

"Oh well, supposing I've made a decision, it could be a couple of weeks in the Caribbean, or maybe a week with my family in Florida."

Example 2:

"Monica, what's you're opinion about the way our early retirement programme is working, and what effect is it having on production?"

Monica's silence means she doesn't want to say anything before consulting with her superiors.

"Suppose it was your decision... what would you do?"

"Well, if it were my decision (which both of you know it isn't) the first thing I'd do would be to..."

And there you are, with the all information you need!

If nothing works... ask yourself if you're really interested in the person

You've equipped yourself with a battery of techniques for getting even the most hardened clam types to open up. However, in a couple of cases all your efforts have failed.

No doubt you still haven't been able to understand how these persons differ from yourself - how they perceive the world differently than you do - and adapt your approach to their specific outlook. Discerning these differences is an art which requires concentration and patient training.

And there may be something else you need to correct. The best way to get someone to open up is to show that you have a real interest in them.

Very often our interest is just a facade. We ask questions without being really interested in the answers. We're more inclined to want to talk about ourselves, and attract attention to ourselves rather than give our time and attention to others.

Clams can invariably detect this. As we've seen, they are usually very sensitive people, who protect themselves by hiding behind a shell. These people will know for certain whether your interest is real or feigned. If it isn't, any technique you use will be a poor substitute for the real thing.

Telephone clams

There are people who, although capable of engaging in normal conversation ninety percent of the time, find themselves speechless when forced to talk on the telephone, even to people they know well.

When we converse - or at least attempt to converse - with these occasional clams, we get the impression we're engaged in a monologue rather than a dialogue, and that everything we say is going in one ear and out the other. We feel even more ridiculous than when this happens face to face.

At least with the person in front of us, we can tell from his / her expression and body language that what we are saying is being registered. But on the phone, we can't even be sure of that.

Why do telephones create clams?

In the great majority of cases, telephone clams are people who lack self confidence, who are timid and introverted, who have to make a great effort just to assert themselves and acquire a minimum of self assurance.

So although they give the impression of not having a communication problem, as soon as they find themselves holding a telephone receiver they seem to be overcome, once again, by the shyness and clumsiness they've taken so much pains to hide.

Shyness is usually a manifestation of a person's fear of rejection or ridicule. That's why shy people, although they may have learned to assert themselves with others, need the constant reassurance of their listeners, in the form of subtle body language and approving gestures, to maintain their confidence.

You can guess the rest.

The telephone eliminates all these subtle forms of communication. The clam cannot see the person on the other end of the line. This provokes a regression into silence.

What can you do to make them talk?

The first part of your strategy remains the same - ask open ended questions which cannot be answered in monosyllables. Since you cannot accompany the question with an interested and inquisitive look, try to express your interest in the tone of your voice. In other words, make your voice more expressive than it would be in a face to face conversation.

You can also accompany your question with a more insistent statement such as: "I'd really like to hear your opinion on this subject…" or "I place a lot of value on your opinion…" or "I'm counting on your comments…" and so on.

Once you've asked the question, give the person some time to organise his / her thoughts, and then ask it again if no answer is forth coming.

What to do if the person on the other end remains silent?

As we've already said, you must avoid getting upset at all cost. Don't make any aggressive remarks. If you do, the result will be the opposite of what you want, and you may turn the person into a permanent clam, instead of an occasional one, as far as you're concerned.

For both your sakes, avoid aggravating the situation in this way. This doesn't mean you should let the person hang up without getting what you want. Make it clear that you intend to call back after allowing the person time to organise his / her thoughts.

Set up an appointment for a follow up call, and suggest that the person's present unwillingness to respond can be put down to the circumstances (emotional shock, surprise, being unprepared, etc.) but that these excuses will not be accepted next time.

As a last resort, insist on meeting the person face to face. Personal encounters will make communicating a lot easier for both of you!

Your training programme

As you can imagine, listening to advice on how to communicate with clam types isn't enough. To learn how to really deal with this category of "difficult" people, you have to practice.

Discerning the predominant sensory input in others

It's important to know what your predominating sense is: visual, auditory or tactile. We're leaving out the olfactory and taste senses because they very rarely predominate in humans.

However, in certain cases (chefs, wine tasters, perfume manufacturers, etc.) the sense of taste or smell may very well be the principle way these people relate to the world, and you may have to orient your communication accordingly.

But such cases are unusual, and to simplify your training we've limited ourselves to the three primary senses - sight, hearing and touch.

Once you've detected a person's dominant sense, you simply have to make an effort to speak the same language as they do.

Easier said than done, you may be thinking. And you're right. Difficult to do, but by no means impossible, and well worth the effort, since accomplishing this will make you an excellent and effective communicator.

What problems are involved?

There are two main problems you will encounter. The first is in learning to recognise a person's dominant sense. The second is learning to express yourself using different language than you would ordinarily.

At the end of this book, you'll find an "Appendix To Chapter 4" consisting of two self-diagnostic tests.

The first will help you determine what your dominant sense is. It's called V.A.S. (Visual - Auditory - Sensory) Test. Respond as you would to a magazine test or survey - in other words as spontaneously as possible. The aim of the test is above all to make you more aware of the dimensions of your personality, not to define it conclusively. To do that would require a lot more testing and analysis.

To get an idea of the dominant sense in the people around you, make photocopies of the test and get them to complete it. They'll acquire a better understanding of themselves, and you'll understand why communicating with them may sometimes have been difficult in the past. This can only improve your relations at home and at work.

The second test - "Filters" - will help you determine the main criteria you use to sort information.

What if you could now ask a person who refuses to talk to you to complete the V.A.S. and Filter tests? I'll bet that doing these exercises together would represent a large step forward in improving your communication.

If you can't use the test

Obviously you can't take the V.A.S. test with you wherever you go, and ask people to complete it whenever the need arises. Fortunately there are other ways to determine people's dominant sense.

Some methods require an in-depth understanding of applied psychology, and are not within the framework of this work.

However, there are others which are easier to learn, and which I will now describe.

Choice of words reflect the dominant sense

The first thing you should be aware of is that the words we use are a direct reflection of our predominant sense. So all you have to do is pay attention to the words a person uses.

Let's go back to the example we looked at previously, of persons speaking a different language:

Martine: "I'm listening to you, but I don't know what you're talking about. It really makes no sense to me."

Mark: "Can't you see what I'm doing! I'm trying to use a little imagination to get you to understand what I mean."

Violet: "I really don't feel you're making sense either. Your images just leaves me cold." In your opinion, what are their dominant senses?

Martine:	(auditory)
Mark:	(visual)
Violet:	(tactile)

And when I say something like, "This sounds like a conversation between deaf mutes..." what sense am I evoking? Hearing, of course. The fact that I use this expression is not due to chance.

It shows that hearing is my dominant sense. I could have said something like, "They need someone to spell it out for them..." (visual) or "You can cut through the tension between them with a cake knife..." (tactile).

People who are exposed to this technique for the first time may find it difficult to believe that just because someone says, "Look at this... I want to show you something..." we have irrefutable proof that the person is visually oriented. They think that the person is simply making use of a common expression that anyone - auditory or tactile oriented persons included - could use. That is not the case. Using this expression is a sure indication of the person's dominant sense.

Of course you'll always find exceptions. Some people contradict themselves constantly, others have been forced to use a different language than the one they would naturally choose - a visual person may have been conditioned in school to think in auditory terms - the same way some left-handed children are forced to write with their right hand.

Characteristic words

To help you determine a person's dominant sense, here is a list of words and expressions which characterise each sense: VISUAL: Perspective - point of view - watch over -keep an eye on - show - my mind is a blank - look this over - point out - illustrate - look familiar - take another look - enlighten - blinded - symmetry - brilliant - I don't see it that way...

Add as many more characteristically visual words and expressions as you can think of: AUDITORY: I hear what you're saying - listen to your comments - rings a bell - listen to me - I'm going to explain something to you - that doesn't strike a chord - I'm speechless - silence - harmonious - I'm listening - help me understand - forgot to mention - the long and the short of it is - I'd like to refer to - talking to a stone - fall on deaf ears - an echo of a response...

Add as many more characteristically auditory words and expressions as you can think of: TACTILE: Have a feeling - a premonition - stick to - vibrate - insensitive to - heavy - gloomy - striking - take care - put my finger on it - take matters in hand - seize control - put the pressure on - tighten the screws - warm / cold atmosphere - soft - rough - emotion - gut feeling - get things moving - sad - in depth...

Add as many more characteristically tactile words and expressions as you can think of:

NON-SPECIFIC:

Not all words in a language refer clearly to one of the five senses. Some are non-specific - i.e. they give no clear indication of a person's dominant sense. Here are a few examples of such words:

Attitude - consider - persevere - perception - reveal - emit - absent - simple - ostentatious - attentive - ignore - expose - note - go beyond - identify - conceive - repeat - remember... etc.

Add as many more characteristically non-specific words and expressions as you can think of:

Analyse a conversation to determine its V.A.S.

You now have the information you need to determine, through words and expressions, the dominant sensory input of a person.

The best way to practice this technique is to note down key words while listening to someone speak. You won't be able to do this while engaged in a conversation yourself, unless the other person is informed, and agrees to participate in the exercise.

So you can use television interviews, or conversations you overhear in a restaurant, or on the public transit. You can also ask friends or relatives to tell you about trips they took, or films they saw, etc.

You then note down key words and expressions that the person uses (unless you're a stenographer, in which case you can record the whole monologue) as follows:

"Trip to Brittany... wind whistling over... height of the cliffs... tremendous silence at night... the chanting in the churches on Sunday... the whisper of the ocean... I said to myself - This is where I want to live..."

I hope the example is clear to you - obviously we're dealing with an auditory person here. As you can see, you don't have to fill pages and pages with your notes. Sometimes all you need are two or three sentences to determine a person's dominant sense.

At other times a person may use a lot of non-specific expressions, or mix visual, auditory and tactile terms so that you aren't sure which is dominant. In such cases you have to be patient and analyse the language more carefully.

Exercise: Moving from one language to another

A good way to practice a language that isn't your own is to take a simple story like "Little Red Riding Hood" and repeat it out loud, concentrating on one set of sensory inputs each time.

Visual: Once there was a little girl with golden blonde hair and rosy cheeks, wearing a grey, pleated skirt and a blouse with little white and blue checks...

Auditory: She heard her mother's voice calling her from the kitchen. Then her mother's footsteps pounded in the hallway, and her mother burst into the room shouting, "Do you have to be so noisy!"

Tactile: Little Red Riding Hood grabbed up her basket and sighed. She tested the cake her mother had put in it with her hand - it felt a little warm. The idea of taking a walk through the forest made her feel happy with expectation.

Olfactory: The smell her mother's special perfume made her aware that her mother was standing beside her. She breathed in the wonderful kitchen odours, then sniffed her fingers to make sure they didn't smell of garlic, and asked her mother if she could try some jam.

Gustatory: Her mother's jam was incomparably delicious. It had the fruity savour of freshly picked berries, slightly sour. Even thinking about it made her mouth water, and she thought of all the wonderful things she'd be eating at her Grandmother's house.

There you are - just continue the story in the same order: visual, auditory, tactile, olfactory, and gustatory. I don't know a better way to practice using the different sensory aspects of language.

Recognising categories of information- sorting

As we've said, human beings see reality in different ways, emphasising one aspect over others. To find out what category you fall into, complete the "Filter Test" in the appendix at the end of this book. Like the V.A.S. Test, no reflection or calculation is required - just answer as spontaneously as possible.

You'll probably be surprised by how accurate the results are. Make copies of this test too, and distribute them to friends, colleagues and family, and especially to any clam types you can persuade.

If you can't use the test...

To find out what a person's principle information sorting criteria is, you have to listen attentively to what they say. The filter he or she uses will quickly become apparent.

Certain persons only talk about other people. Others concentrate on places, others provide very precise information. The same method you used for determining a dominant sense also applies here - just note down key words and expressions during the course of a conversation, a televised interview, a speech, etc.

Asking some one to tell you about one of the most beautiful days in their lives is a good way to find out what that person's information sorting filter is.

Was it when s/he got a new car (object)? Was it on the occasion of a party with good friends (people)? Was it an important event, like a graduation or an award ceremony? Does the person provide a lot of detailed information about who was there, what gifts s/he received, how much they cost, etc. (objects)? Or was it related to a particularly beautiful sunset in some exotic place (location)? Did it have to do with being the first to climb a mountain (activity)?

You'll probably notice that few people use only one information sorting filter. They usually appear in pairs. Others may be present, but of secondary importance.

Some criteria will be totally ignored, and that's where problems can arise. Imagine that objects are extremely important to you, while your spouse places hardly any importance on objects at all. This could lead to serious misunderstandings!

Adapt to the different criteria of the people around you

This exercise consists of thinking of ways to present a project to someone by using arguments that appeal to each of the six filters for sorting information.

To "sell" the trip to Greece, for example, what would you say to someone whose emphasis is on:

- events
- locations

- actions
- people
- information
- objects

Some categories could prove very troublesome, especially those you don't relate to at all. Get someone to help you if necessary. Other people will be only too happy to show you how to speak their language, and they may also want to make the effort to learn yours!

CHAPTER 5
Verbal Ping Pong or The Dangers of Playing Offense

The example of the golden bracelet

John and Susan have been married for ten years. John is a manager in a private company, Susan is a nurse, working for a fairly low salary. A year ago, the couple agreed to cut their family spending so that John could take off one day a week and go back to school.

Their marriage anniversary was coming up. In the past they'd celebrated the event in a good restaurant, but this year Susan decided to surprise her husband with a meal at home.

She started looking through recipe books for something sumptuous, but inexpensive. She bought some material to make a present for her husband - a new bathrobe. She even bought some perfumed candles from a friend, to help make the evening a special occasion.

Finally, the day of their anniversary arrived. Proud of her work, Susan barely got everything finished before her husband came home from work.

He breezed in, all excited, saying, "Honey, tonight we're going out! I made reservations at that new restaurant downtown. The hell with our budget! We're going to live it up for a change!"

"Wait a minute," Susan led him to the dining area, lit with candles, a bottle of champagne cooled and ready to open. "Look, I thought we could eat at home tonight." John felt a little reluctant to give up his Santa Claus role. But he agreed to eat at home, knowing that he had another ace up his sleeve.

After the meal, John took a little box wrapped in gold paper out of his pocket and offered it to Susan. She felt a little uneasy as she tore off the wrapping. Inside she found a superb gold bracelet, set with sapphires, exactly like the one she had admired in a shop window a few weeks past.

Tears well up in her eyes. John thinks it's because she's so happy. Feeling very pleased with himself, he tries to take her in his arms. He gets the surprise of his life when Susan pushes him away, and throws the bracelet to the ground.

"How could you!" she cries. "When I look at that damned bracelet, all it makes me think of are the hundred and one things I have to do to save money every week - the damned specials I have to look for to get us proper food, the dresses I can't buy, the vacations we can't take, the way we have to go visit my parents because we haven't got enough money to go anywhere else... And you think you can have fun playing the prince and buying expensive toys because it amuses you, even if it puts us into debt for the next five years!"

John is speechless. He tries to explain that he was just trying to show his gratitude for all the sacrifices she's been making on his behalf, so that he can get the qualifications he needs for a promotion. He gets caught up in defending his actions, and this leads to a long, drawn out quarrel where both sides blame each other for all the little grievances they've been hoarding up over their years of living together.

This is what is called verbal ping pong. It's a dangerous little drama where both sides -consciously or not - hurl hostile messages at each other which are often contradictory and always indirect. Old wounds are opened, new ones are created.

Another example:

Mark is nineteen years old. He lives with his mother, Joanne, and his two younger brothers, aged eight and twelve. Joanne has a full time job, and also takes care of the housework. According to her... "Mark is a really good kid. But I must have told him a hundred times to wipe his feet before coming into the kitchen. He never does, he's always leaving his muddy tracks on the linoleum."

Why?

Joanne is very busy, what with her job, taking care of the kids, and attending all the committees and charities she belongs to. She can't afford to pay a babysitter when she goes out, so Mark is regularly left in charge.

He thinks she goes out too much. But Joanne is well aware of the dangers of being a single mother and cutting off all social activities, so she makes an effort not to lose touch with her old friends. When Mark objects, she accuses him of being selfish. She lets him know.

In fact, children are masters at this game, which often results in a kind of emotional blackmail. Let's listen to what a woman, divorced and living alone with her six year old daughter, has to say about a dinner invitation she extended to a man she is thinking about marrying:

"I put Tina to bed at eight o'clock, and asked her to behave herself while Dennis was here. It turned out to be a horrible evening! She didn't misbehave or start crying or anything like that. That would have been easy! What she did do was call me to her room every five minutes. Either she was thirsty, or she couldn't find her teddy bear, or she wanted me to kiss her goodnight, or she had to tell me how much she loves me, or she was too hot and wanted the window open, and then of course she was too cold... I'm telling you she drove me crazy. It's lucky Dennis likes kids!"

What made Tina act this way? Quite simply, it was her fear of being rejected. And this feeling, although so obvious (since as a child Tina was not as adept at hiding her real feelings as adults are when engaged in this game of verbal ping pong) was the motivating force behind her, at times, contradictory messages. Her behaviour was a natural reaction to the threat she felt was being directed at her relationship with her mother.

Adults who do not wish to break off a relationship entirely, but who, at the same time, want to change something about the it, send even more indirect messages, hoping to avoid a direct confrontation. This is the case, for example, with couples who criticise each other in public because they are afraid to do so when they're alone.

Let's take another look at our examples...

Mark thinks his mother takes advantage of him, but he doesn't dare come right out and say it because he's afraid of her reaction, of being accused of selfishness and of not loving her.

So he makes an indirect (and unconscious) statement of protest by muddying up the kitchen floor, and then disguises this hostile message in a show of affection.

Joanne is afraid of getting angry with her son, thereby losing his precious help, and so tries to avoid a confrontation as well. She prefers hearing an outwardly positive message (Mark's apologies, hugs and compliments) and agrees to ignore the real negative message (the mud on the kitchen floor).

In John and Susan's case, Susan thinks that:

- all her sacrifices and efforts to manage the household on a reduced budget were not important;
- her husband doesn't care, or takes her efforts for granted - they are nothing to be proud of;
- her husband's manly pride and his need to be the breadwinner in the family made him go out and splurge on a luxurious gift they couldn't afford, with no thought of tomorrow.

As for John, frustrated in his role of benefactor, he pretends to see Susan as an ungrateful wife, embittered by the financial sacrifices she's had to make over the last year, and ultimately unworthy of the magnificent present he bought her.

John and Susan are not on the same wavelength. Their line of communication has been broken. But, fearing to destroy the relationship completely, neither is capable of saying openly what they think about their respective attitudes.

Terrified at the idea of confronting the real problem, they prefer to make indirect accusations and open old wounds, thinking (completely erroneously) that they'll be hurting each other less by doing so.

Isn't it tempting to adopt the philosophy of an eye for an eye? When verbal ping pong has become the normal mode of communication in a relationship, both parties become victims of each other's hostility.

What are the results of this dangerous game?

Unfortunately, the end result is often precisely what both sides are trying to avoid - i.e. the end of the relationship. The only other alternative is that both sides accept the game of verbal ping pong as their normal way of life, and remain together, while continually accusing each other of being "difficult" people.

Both sides bare their claws, say and do terrible things to each other, which they then try to patch up with shows of affection, but which only poison their lives completely. Being together becomes mutually aggravating, and finally intolerable. Any compromise or negotiation becomes impossible, and the relationship breaks apart.

Even if the situation doesn't deteriorate to that point, the relationship suffers. Sometimes couples get into the habit of avoiding any subject that might cause friction, afraid once again of complete rejection and the end of the relationship.

They assume that because one aspect of their behaviour is being rejected, the rest will be rejected as well. This is exactly the way a child thinks: s/he relates any kind of refusal by the parents (buying a toy or going to Disney land) as a total rejection.

Under such conditions, how can a relationship be expected to evolve, to develop and mature? Growth is stymied by all the shadowy grey areas that confine and confuse people's real feelings.

How to remedy this problem?

Are you involved in a similar situation? Do you consider someone close to you "difficult" while knowing full well that s/he thinks the same thing about you?

Do something about it before it's too late. Not only will you save a relationship that's important to you, you'll also find that making an effort in this direction is a perfect occasion for developing your character and self esteem.

You know that both your attitudes stem from a desire for change that neither one of you is able to openly express, because you both fear that doing so will result in a total rejection.

No matter which of you is the dominating force in the relationship, you both feel powerless to effect a change.

Let's tale another look at one of our examples: Joanne, although she is Mark's mother and ostensibly the head of the family, is afraid of the way her son will react if she forces him to wipe his feet before entering the kitchen. She's afraid to lose his help in caring for the other children, which she desperately needs.

So in this kind of "difficult" relationship, neither side takes the initiative and makes the desired changes.

Here are some steps to follow to remedy this, or a similar situation:

1. Become aware of the problem

To start, you have to determine the circumstances that are likely to develop into a game of verbal ping pong. Ask yourself a few questions.

But be careful! Don't fall into the trap of trying to read the other person's mind. Become aware of YOUR problems. It's hard enough dealing with your own mind, believe me!

Ask yourself what is bothering you, why you tend to react in a certain way, and what circumstances unconsciously seem to provoke this type of negative reaction. Do the following exercise, which may be aptly termed an "examination of the subconscious."

Exercise: Examining your subconscious

- Get comfortable, with a pen and paper handy.
- Try to recall at least two recent arguments you had with the person in question.
- Remember the exact circumstances. Try to analyse your feelings at those moments. What provoked your animosity? Be honest with yourself. Hide absolutely nothing.
- Write down everything you felt, openly and frankly.

It's important that you use the first person "I" when making your notes, to emphasise the fact that you're talking about yourself.

"Yesterday I felt like a victim in my relationship with Sally. I felt ripped off and betrayed when she accused me of being dishonest..." etc.

Write only precise facts and your feelings. You'll be the only one to read what you write. This process of analysis will help you see yourself more clearly. In addition, writing your feelings down on paper will help you gain some objectivity towards what happened, and in so doing take the drama out of the confrontation.

2. Don't allow a relationship to deteriorate

As soon as you feel a relationship is starting to turn sour and realise that the other person is saying or doing things that upset you, don't wait - remove the infection immediately!

You may be thinking that it's impossible to take these precautions every time someone says or does something unpleasant. How do you know when the right time has come to express your negative feelings, instead of just letting things pass?

What happens is that in a relationship that isn't working, both sides accumulate negative points. At first, they don't amount to much, and you can let them pass without reacting. But the event sticks in your memory, whether you like it or not.

Then another incident occurs. You decide that it isn't serious enough for an out and out confrontation, and let it pass once again. However, a second negative point is added to the first.

As time passes, more incidents occur, some more serious than others, and each one adds to your collection of thorns. And then one day something happens that breaks the camel's back. It may be a minor incident, not half as serious as some of the things that already happened, and which you let pass, but it's is the last straw and you blow your top.

This process is well known to anyone who has lived through a relationship, and has been studied closely by psychologists. They've come up with a formula which advises people to: "Never go to sleep bearing a grudge towards someone."

A variation of this rule is: "Never let more than six hours pass before clearing up your resentment towards someone."

Never let a problem grow to the point where it infects the relationship. The hostile messages directed at you are really calls for help. Don't respond by being aggressive and perpetuating the vicious circle.

An example

Unfortunately, our example concerns a situation which is still quite common among couples.

Marilyn and Jack had their first child two years ago. Marilyn gave up her job as a clothes designer. It was a job she liked a lot, but Jack, as well as all her in-laws, insisted she stop working and stay home to take care of the baby. Marilyn was afraid to refuse. Doing so would have made her appear callous, unworthy to be a mother, and ungrateful to her husband. She suppressed her feelings of disappointment and her growing lack of self esteem.

Jack would come home every night, full of stories about what happened at the office. He was very enthusiastic about his job. Marilyn, meanwhile, sought for ways (unconsciously and indirectly) to vent her unhappiness. She forgot to call the plumber to fix a leak; she lost the car keys; she accepted invitations to events she knew her husband wouldn't enjoy; she made sure to be out when he came home from work...etc.

She unconsciously looked for ways to annoy him, without going so far as to provoke a direct confrontation.

Jack admires his wife's many qualities, but considers her a little "difficult" to handle at times. But since he's so comfortable in his traditional role of male breadwinner, with his wife twiddling her thumbs at home, he doesn't want to ask any direct questions that may upset the status quo.

Deep down, he knows that Marilyn is unhappy, that she feels confined and unappreciated. But he absolutely doesn't want to be the one to confront the issue by asking questions.

How can Marilyn and Jack solve their problem? Actually, all they need to do is sit down and have a frank discussion. They should first analyse their personal problems separately, and then negotiate with each other. Unfortunately, both of them are afraid to jeopardise the relationship.

That's why Jack responds to Marilyn's behavioural quirks with a kind of irritated indulgence. Marilyn, in turn, responds to her husband's "superiority" with seemingly insignificant, yet repeated acts of petty revenge.

They are both slowly poisoning each other's existence.

Don't follow their example!

In this situation, Marilyn is afraid to complain that taking care of the baby full time bores her, and that she misses her work. As for Jack, nothing will make him admit that he's afraid of giving up his gratifying role of "provider" and head of the family.

To save the relationship, one of them has to bring the problem out in the open. Marilyn will probably be the one to do so, since she seems to be more aware of her feelings than Jack, and will probably have less difficulty expressing herself. In addition, she's the one who feels victimised.

3. Share your feelings

You may be asking yourself how you can be sure that negative points are accumulating in a relationship. Well, it's very simple: when you're communicating with someone, you leave the person feeling content, energised, serene. These are signs that the relationship is working well.

When communication is unsatisfactory, your exchanges leave you feeling heavy and somehow empty. These are danger signs, and you should act immediately to restore harmony and balance.

I remember an incident that happened to me, shortly after I studied the principles that I'm explaining to you now.

One of my best friends phoned me to tell me that he urgently needed to borrow a large sum of money. I happened to have just enough money in my savings account at the time, and I didn't need to use it right away. However, I knew that I'd be needing the money in a month, and that if I didn't have it back by then I'd be in serious trouble. So I offered to lend my friend the money, on condition that he pay me back by the end of the month. He agreed, promising he would do so.

Say "No" without destroying a relationship

When I put the phone down after saying "yes" to my friend's request, I felt overcome with anxiety. The assurances he'd given me for returning the money on time were not realistic. I knew he'd been having money problems for awhile, and that it was highly probable he wouldn't be able to pay me back on time.

In the name of friendship, I'd agreed to something that I didn't feel comfortable with. So there I was, pensive, worried, sitting next to the phone, thinking about all the problems my decision would cause. My discomfort was a sure sign that I'd come out a loser in the exchange with my friend. I had to do something to rectify the situation.

I thought about my friend and his money problems. My offer of help had probably taken a great burden off his mind. How could I tell him I'd changed my mind, without losing his friendship?

Well, here's where the golden rule applies: "Never let more than six hours pass without..." And if I was going to lose a friend, I'd rather it was because I didn't lend him the money than because he couldn't pay it back!

So I called him back. I explained why I felt uneasy about my decision. I talked about my problem, and the fact that I didn't want it to destroy our friendship. And then I explained that it was for that reason that I wasn't going to lend him the money.

Would you believe me if I told you that we've remained the best of friends? He valued our friendship as much as I did, and didn't want to destroy it either. He appreciated my frankness, which was further proof of my affection for him. He didn't want to create problems for me, so he went and found someone else to borrow the money from who wasn't under the same pressure as I was.

Take the risk of showing your vulnerability

I'd like you to try your hand at being frank and open the next time an occasion arises. You have everything to gain, and nothing to lose!

If you are unable to be frank with someone, it's because you're afraid of being rejected. You fear losing the love of a person who is close to you if you don't play the role expected of you - i.e. a kind, generous, devoted, understanding person, even though you may find this role confining, and feel terribly exploited.

What would happen if you suddenly revealed what you're really thinking? If you told the person that you aren't really as generous, patient, kind, devoted and understanding as you've been made out to be?

People who place a lot of importance on projecting a perfect image should not expect others to like them more for it. As the saying goes, "Perfection is not of this world..."

People who demand perfection are difficult to live with

In its absolute sense, perfection is inhuman, and those who pretend to be perfect or demand perfection from others (the two often go hand in hand) are very difficult to take. They represent a perpetual threat of being found lacking, and of subsequently being rejected because of our inability to live up to their expectations.

We have to recognise the value of our own, and other people's imperfections - the little faults and weaknesses that make us human. Being vulnerable and imperfect brings us closer to other people, since it allows them to lower their own masks and reveal themselves as they really are.

Being close to someone only becomes possible when you set aside your defences, which means that you accept your vulnerability instead of trying to hide it. Only then can a joyous exchange between two people occur - when you no longer have to play a role in order to hide your real self, and your needs.

This is the paradox of being vulnerable. The more we believe we are weak and worthless, the more we need to hide our faults and project an artificially enhanced image of our person, convinced that this is the only way to gain the confidence and respect of others.

The more confident we are of our own worth, the more able we are to recognise our faults and imperfections, and the less we need to hide them. We know that nothing can make us lose the affection of those who really love us.

This is true for individuals. It also holds true for organisations and countries. It is a well known fact that the more a political regime refuses to recognise its errors, the weaker it appears to be.

So you have everything to gain by revealing your vulnerability to others, and letting them know that you fear being rejected by them, and esteem their respect and affection. Doing so will certainly improve the stability of your relationships.

Overcome the obstacle of resentment

As we've seen, during a verbal ping pong situation, all kinds of things come to the surface that have been accumulating over time. Each reproach stems from some kind of frustration, some incident which has been suppressed into a bitter memory. The accumulation of frustration builds a tremendous amount of resentment, which finally explodes. And this explosion only serves to feed our feelings of hate and resentment, creating a very vicious circle which, fortunately, is possible to break.

The anatomy of resentment

The phenomenon is not hard to understand. It is produced every time an action does not correspond to an expectation.

Say for example that your child is rude to you. Well, you wouldn't want your child to be totally docile and nice all the time either. If you were able to accept his / her behaviour as being completely normal (maybe rudeness runs in the family) or if you could love him / her despite this fault, then the child's behaviour would produce absolutely no feelings of animosity or resentment in you.

This doesn't mean you have to like it. But you can tolerate it, like you tolerate the cold weather in winter, or a minor grippe. It wouldn't make any sense to accumulate resentment against the winter elements, would it!

Resentment is born of expectation

Resentment is something that arises in you because you have expectations. When I work with a group of people, I am sometimes a little impatient. Some people find this stimulating and even thank me for it. Others complain because they think I should be gentle and patient all the time...

We have an ideal image of the way we think other people should behave, in the same way that they have an ideal image of us. The problem is knowing to what point we should try to conform to other people's expectations.

Psychologists have found an answer to this problem. One thing is certain: there's nothing that obliges us to fulfil other people's expectations. We have our own expectations, and so do they. What is essential to a healthy relationship is being able to communicate about the subject of our expectations, so that both sides know what they're up against.

Then everything becomes a question of compatibility and negotiation. I'll make an effort if you will too - then maybe we can both be winners in this relationship.

Who does your resentment hurt?

Say you've allowed a lot of negative points to accumulate in your relations with certain people. You've patiently catalogued your frustrations, and these have gradually formed into a compact little ball of heavy, vicious, bitter, smelly and ugly matter, that you carry with you permanently. This ball of poison is your resentment.

It's time to become aware, if you haven't already done so, that YOU are the one your resentment is hurting the most. The person you feel resentment against may not even know about it!

This means you are twice a loser: first because of the initial frustration or disappointment you felt; and second because you have to carry these negative feelings around, and suffer all the associated consequences. Yet there are people who would rather die than give up their resentment. There is even hatred that is transmitted from one generation to another, so that in time people find they know who to hate, even though they've forgotten why!

An example:

Ben's boss is a tyrant, a despot with a mean streak, who runs his department like a slave driver, dominating and sometimes hurting his colleagues without even being aware of what he's doing, running over everyone like a bull in a china shop.

Even thinking about his boss sets Ben's little ball of resentment throbbing. He really hates the guy, and he's not the only one at the office who does. But this hatred is poisoning Ben's life. He really has to make an effort to go to work every morning, and every time his boss asks him to do something, he grumbles and reluctantly obeys.

Ben has been in a continual bad mood since his new boss was appointed, and the negative repercussions are starting to show up in his personal life. He loses patience with his wife and children a lot more easily, and the atmosphere when he's around is always heavy and tense.

He's even finding it difficult to sleep, obsessed as he is with finding ways to vent his resentment, although he never actually does anything about it. He's becoming impossible to live with, his resentment is devouring him, and ruining his health to boot. What will happen to him if he isn't cured of this disease?

Ben's boss, meanwhile, isn't losing any sleep. His conscience is clean. He's not even aware that there's anything wrong with the way he treats his subordinates. In fact, he's noticed that some of the people in his department are very hard to get along with. Especially Ben, who seems to be so negative all the time... he's not sure he'll be able to keep him on staff.

In your opinion, who is going to suffer more from Ben's resentment - Ben or his boss?

How to free yourself of resentment

The remedy for resentment is as simple as the anatomy of the problem itself. Since resentment results from actions which do not correspond to what we expect from some idealised image of a person, all we have to do is change the action, or change the image.

If we look at our example, this leaves Ben with two options:

Change the behaviour

Ben can set to work trying to change the behaviour - i.e. the actions - of his boss by letting him know that there's a problem with the way he treats his employees. If no one has ever mentioned anything before, Ben's boss may very well have been acting with the best intentions in the world, in which case he'll be very happy that someone has finally been honest enough to bring the problem to his attention.

Try to think of people you know who attract resentment without being aware it. Don't you think you'd be doing them a service by letting them know that there's something wrong with their behaviour? I've known people like this, who have been able to improve their relations considerably, after being told what they were doing to upset people.

Change the image

I've also known people who have refused to change, despite all the hints they were given. They think that it's other people's responsibility to adapt to them, and not vice versa. It's a question of point of view, and of power. This is where the second option becomes useful - change the image.

In Ben's case, it's highly unlikely that he'll be able to change his boss' behaviour. So he has to live with resentment, which as we saw is pushing him towards an early and unexpected retirement. He can also work on accepting his boss the way he is.

After all, where did he get the idea that a boss has to be understanding, generous and equitable? Does anyone's boss really live up to this image completely? Does Ben himself practice the virtues he demands from his boss?

You can see that it wouldn't take much to transform these terrible feelings of resentment into a simple disagreement over the way the department personnel should be handled, which would be a lot easier to live with.

What to do when the situation has been going on for a long time?

It is possible to change an action which causes resentment as it's happening. My neighbour drives me crazy every Sunday morning, cutting wood for his fireplace with a power saw. I can take the necessary steps to get him to stop, or arrange to be absent from home at that time.

But what can I do about an injustice I was subjected to ten years ago, by someone I haven't seen since, but for whom I still feel such resentment, it's as if the event happened yesterday?

Can I do anything to change the original action? No, the harm is done, and there's no way I can go back and demand an apology or compensation.

Can I change my image? No, I could never consider what that person did to me as acceptable behaviour. It was much too serious.

Then what? Am I condemned to live with this ball of resentment to the end of my days? Is it true that only time can heal my wounds?

This is a problem which has preoccupied people since ancient times, and various powerful remedies, both religious and social, have been found. The importance of forgiveness and reconciliation is central in Christian tradition, and people whose faith is strong enough to find a solution in the concept Christian forgiveness are fortunate.

For the rest of us, there are a number of purely psychological processes which can do a lot to alleviate the pressures of longstanding resentments. One example will be described at the end of this chapter.

Your training programme

Situations involving bouts of verbal ping pong and people you find difficult because of barriers of resentment, are fertile ground for putting counter measures into practice. The following training programme can show you how to radically transform the panorama of your interpersonal relations.

Work on resentment

A. Take a sheet of paper. Make a list of ALL persons you know,

or have known, against whom you feel the even slightest resentment. If you have any negative feelings or thoughts when you think of someone, add her / his name to the list.

B. For each of the persons on your list, answer the following questions: - What is the cause of my resentment towards this person? - Which of my expectations were not fulfilled by this person? - Is there anything I can do about this situation (change my image of the person, satisfy my demands... etc.)? - How can I put an end to my resentment? Write down your answers, and then put them into practice.

Clean up your communication act

One way to be sure of getting involved in verbal ping pong matches in future is not to take care of your responsibilities, however minor they may appear. This is only logical if you consider that by accepting a responsibility, you create an expectation, and by not taking care of it you are provoking feelings of frustration.

Here is a list of areas which may be sources of negative points, and which you can easily do something about: - Take care of all your outstanding communication (messages you didn't send, letters or thank you notes you forgot to write, visits you promised to make and didn't, etc.) - Make apologies for all responsibilities or engagements you didn't keep (returning a book, taking someone out for dinner, helping someone with housecleaning, etc.) - Clear up any imprecise, vague areas in your communication. (Being vague leads to lying through omission. For example, you forget to mention that you got a raise in salary, or that you took someone out for dinner, etc.) - Write all the letters you have to, or have been meaning to write. - Stop being secretive, telling lies and pretending about things in areas where you feel confident enough to show your vulnerability.

Preparing for reconciliation

Here is the way you should approach a meeting destined to reconcile your differences with someone. If you think it will help you, prepare for the meeting ahead of time, by writing down the things you want to say. This will prevent you from forgetting anything in the heat of the moment.

- Clearly explain your fear of rejection.

- If the other person refuses to open up to you, explain your feelings in detail.

- Use the same format as you would for analysing your subconscious - i.e. speak using the first person "I" to make it clear that you're talking about yourself only.

- Above all, don't try to read the other person's mind. Don't put words into his / her mouth. There's nothing more exasperating than listening to someone say, "Oh yes, I know exactly what you're thinking…"

- Don't forget to state clearly that the friendship or affection you feel for the other person is not being questioned.

- Finally, recognise your own failings and weaknesses, and show the other person that you are indeed vulnerable.

The process of forgiveness

Real forgiveness is a feeling of acceptance, stripped of all animosity. It is not simply a question of forgetting or negating the sufferings and wrongs of the past. Real forgiveness means remembering without experiencing any negative emotion - serenely and harmoniously.

Some religions suggest a much more radical type of forgiveness, where you learn to replace hate with love, and are finally able to love your enemy. This isn't what we're suggesting here. The process we are describing is purely psychological, and has nothing to do with religious faith.

As you can imagine, being able to regard past events calmly and serenely requires a profound inner transformation which is very difficult to realise on your own, without any outside assistance.

The process I am suggesting is very powerful, if used under the right circumstances. It has to be done in a state of deep relaxation, which this text will teach you. To do this you'll need the help of another person - someone who can read the text to you in an appropriate voice and at the right speed. Or you can get hold of a tape recorder and record the text yourself, or order a prepared version from the publisher of this book.

Relaxation and visualisation exercise

Get into a comfortable position - avoid crossed arms or legs. Close your eyes and concentrate on your eyelids, and more particularly on the little muscles around your eyes. Relax these muscles slowly... very slowly. Now let this feeling of relaxation spread to your whole body. Breathe in deeply, and while breathing repeat the number 7 over and over in your mind, and imagine you're seeing the colour red.

Relax your entire body, from head to toe. Re-lax. Let your body relax... completely.

Now breathe in deeply again, this time repeating the number 6, and visualise the colour orange.

You only want to do what is good for you.

Breathe in deeply. Then as you breathe out repeat the number 5 in your mind, and visualise the colour yellow. Your mind is calm and tranquil. Your mind is at rest. Breathe in deeply again, and as you breathe out repeat the number 4 in your mind, and visualise the colour green. You are overcome by a feeling of peace. Think of the word se-re-ni-ty.

Breathe in deeply, and as you breathe out repeat the number 3 to yourself, while imagining the colour blue. A feeling of love grows from deep within you. You feel full of love.

Breathe in deeply, and as you breathe out repeat the number 2 in your mind, and visualise the colour indigo. You are in touch with the real essence of your being. You are in harmony with yourself.

Breathe in deeply, and as you breathe out repeat the number 1 and visualise the colour violet. You are now in touch with the deepest part of your being, your mind has reached its most profound level. You can use this energy to accomplish whatever you wish, provided that this action is is just and something you sincerely desire.

Now use your creative imagination to visualise a large sphere of white light. This sphere is floating above your head, and emits a beautiful golden white light which bathes your entire body. Let the light penetrate and fill you completely. The golden light fills you, and surrounds you and protects. Only beneficial things can happen to you now, and you release all the negativity and resentment that is being flushed out of your system by this process.

Now visualise yourself in a peaceful, natural setting. Calm yourself... experience a feeling of great tranquillity and harmony with your surroundings. What colours do you see? What kind of plants are growing around you? You fill your lungs with sweet smelling, fresh, pure air. Listen to the sounds. Maybe you can feel the heat of the sun on your skin, and the soft earth beneath your feet. You see a path leading away into the distance...

You start walking on the path, attentive to everything you perceive: images, sounds, sensations. The path continues on through a forest, and then opens onto a clearing that stretches off across a golden prairie, as far as the eye can see. In front of you is an area enclosed by a man-made barrier - a stone wall or wire fence. You step closer and see a sign hanging on the fence, with the word DUMP printed in large letters.

You peek over the barrier and see a heap of rusted scrap, which looks somehow familiar. You push open a gate and walk in, looking closely at the contents. You examine a pile of garbage. It looks very old. You bend down and take a closer look, and your eye is caught by a particular piece of metal. Concentrate all your attention on this piece of metal... and pick it up.

As you hold the piece of metal and weigh it in your hands, think of a time in your past when you stood somebody up - when you said you were going to do something or go somewhere with someone. Do you remember how the person felt when you didn't come through? Do you remember what s/he said? How did you feel about it? What did you say or do when you broke the agreement?

Now put the piece of scrap metal back where it was and let the memory fade.

From here you move on to other piles of scrap, looking for other pieces of metal. Pick one up... look at it... it reminds you of something you did a very long time ago, which you felt guilty about... something you knew you shouldn't have done, but which you did anyway... Were any other persons involved? Did you hurt anybody by your actions? How did you feel? What has happened to your guilt since then?

Put the piece of metal back where you found it, and let the memory fade.

You continue walking around the dump, inspecting the various mounds of garbage. You may be reminded of a time when you were the one who got hurt, when you felt a great deal of resentment towards someone. Maybe you judged or punished someone unfairly, or maybe you were the one judged and punished. You may recall moments of intense hate, anger, sadness, depression. You may think of all the times you were disappointed by others... and of all the resentment you feel towards them.

As you walk through the dump, you detect a faint but foul odour. You look around, and discover that the smell seems to be coming from a separate part of the dump, enclosed by its own wall. You walk up to the wall, but it's too high for you to see over. You find an old wooden crate, and use it to stand on. What you see on the other side of the wall is a very unsavoury pile of garbage indeed - in fact a stinking mess of decomposing matter. And you realise that this smelly heap contains all the things that have been bothering you, nagging at you... things you've rejected or suppressed or hidden... all your animosity, resentment and hate. You knew these things were there... you knew how foul they smelled, and you punished yourself because they were a part of your life. Now just be aware of them - the wall hiding this abominable heap of garbage is the same wall you set up between yourself and others...

Now you move off into a part of the dump that's on slightly higher ground. From there you can see beyond its boundaries. You see something in the distance that seems to be shining softly... it looks attractive and reassuring. This distant place is surrounded by a halo of blue light, with points of purple and gold. This is where the purest part of your mind resides. But at the moment, there is a pile of garbage between you and this pure place, as well as a wall that bars access to this most profound and positive part of yourself.

The time has come to do something about your garbage. You walk away from the inner wall, out through the gate of the dump, and far enough away to take it all in at once. You sit down on the ground and look at the dump from this perspective... remembering all the pain, the punishments, the wounds... all the judgments you made about others that caused them pain and suffering. It's all there in that dump. Imagine that the dump starts turning slowly at first, then faster and faster, transforming into a huge, indistinct mass of dark red matter. All your garbage, the fence, the inner wall, the heaps of scrap, blend together into this huge dark red mass that seems to vibrate...

Now start the healing process. As the dark red mass grows ever more compact, you become aware that it is composed of certain actions you have committed, and of certain things that happened to you... but that the mass is not really you. You know that there is a much deeper place inside you... that place shining softly in the distance - a place of comfort and warmth...

From this shining place, a ray of light projects into the sombre mass of your garbage - a ray which stems from your profound desire for reconciliation. The dark red mass grows a little lighter as the ray penetrates. The mass of negative energy becomes orange. As it grows even lighter, you feel that some of the emotions it contains are dissipating, and you feel lighter. The mass of negative energy continues pulsating and getting lighter in hue. Now it turns yellow. You understand that a great number of the negative events you've experienced were steps on your path to understanding - if you hadn't lived them, you would not understand what you do now. They were meant to open you mind, and help you discover yourself...

As you think about this, the yellow mass turns pale green. Everything becomes even clearer. You understand so much more, and you feel reconciled with yourself. The green colour seems to produce a deep feeling of calm, which pervades your entire body. Reconciliation and forgiveness are easy to achieve. You can now forgive yourself for all the times you judged yourself, and other people, too harshly. And as you experience these feelings of reconciliation and self forgiveness - as you begin to accept yourself - the mass of negative energy takes on a deep blue colour, warm and welcoming... a very beautiful deep blue.

Radiating from this blue colour, a great feeling of sensitivity and solicitude spreads through you... and you start to see tinges of purple.

The negativity in the mass before you has almost completely disappeared, and you are getting closer and closer to that inviting place that is your real self... the place which has always been there to love you and appreciate you... which allowed the dump to exist because it thought you wanted it there.

Now that you've made it disappear, your true self embraces you and welcomes you, happy to have you back again...

The purple colour turns to gold, with a circle of intensely bright white light vibrating at its centre. Now the light is distilled even more purely, and becomes invisible. It fills you up... your heart fills with pure white and golden hued light. Now send the light to all the parts of your body that need healing... to the places where you feel empty, sad, soiled or hurt.

Fill these areas with warm white-golden light. Let the light dissolve any remnants of negativity... of suffering... of need. Let yourself become one with the radiant person you really are...

As you let the light fill your body, let it shine all around you as well, radiating from your heart. Let the light of your love spread out around you, outside of you, first touching, then enveloping and protecting everyone you come in contact with. This is how you can spread the grace of reconciliation, in the form of this beautiful light, all around you...

Now bring your being back to the point where you started out... back to the peaceful clearing where you started using your creative imagination and powers of visualisation.

I'm soon going to ask you to open your eyes. When you do, you will feel completely awake, and in perfect health. Your head and neck will be relaxed. You will feel radiant, and in harmony with life.

When you're ready, you can let yourself become more aware of where you are... of your presence in this place. Feel the contact of the surface you're lying or sitting on. Wiggle your toes. Tighten and relax the muscles in your legs. Move your mouth. Close your fists slowly. Breathe in deeply. Stretch. Open your eyes when you feel ready. You are fully awake, in perfect health. You feel reborn,

You feel charged with renewed energy, and in total harmony with life.

PART TWO

WHAT WEAPONS DO YOU HAVE AT YOUR DISPOSAL?

CHAPTER 6
Four Important Stages

Why proceed in stages?

In our relations with others, we often have to deal with people whose negative personalities cause problems for us: a boss suddenly blows his top about some minor error; a civil servant, comfortably seated behind his / her desk, obstinately refuses to help you; a client who thinks s/he knows more than you do about your work; a spouse who has been suppressing his / her frustration all day at work, comes home and blows off steam at you... and so on.

Whatever type of difficulties you encounter, you need a strategy to deal with them effectively, and make the occasions a cause for success instead of for failure. Here is one such strategy, developed by an American psychologist, Dr. Robert Bramson. I can vouch for its effectiveness personally.

It consists of the following stages:

1. Evaluate the situation.

2. Stop trying to change the other person.

3. Take an objective look at the conflict situation.

4. Adopt a strategy, and stick to it.

You could add a fifth stage to the process, which would consist of analysing the results of your behaviour after the programme has been put into practice. This would allow you to modify aspects of your strategy depending on how well they succeeded.

1. Calmly evaluate the situation by asking yourself some questions

First of all, don't categorise someone as "difficult" just because you have a problem with him or her. As we've already seen, difficult behaviour can be temporary, the result of unusually negative circumstances in a person's life.

This is an important precaution. We tend to blame other people for their faults very quickly, while considering our own mere "human foibles." Whenever a problematic situation arises, we tend to jump to conclusions and classify the other person as "difficult." So the first thing you have to do is make sure you're really confronted with a "difficult" case.

If the situation is unclear, ask yourself a few key questions before labelling someone "difficult" to get along with, and avoid blaming yourself later on, for having made an incorrect assessment.

Here are the key questions you should be asking yourself. We'll examine them one by one.

A. Does the person always react in the same way?

One way of finding out is to discover what triggered the conflict: a remark you made; a remark the other person made; bringing up a delicate subject, etc. If you're honest with yourself, you won't have any trouble putting your finger on the exact words or gestures that led to the conflict.

This will allow you to judge whether the conflict or irritability started with you, or with the other person. You can also check to see if the same circumstance always triggers off the same effect, and if it occurs frequently.

An example:

Jeanette and Charles are biologists. They were chosen to work on a research project together. Right from the start, Jeanette decided her colleague was morose, and didn't have the qualities necessary to work effectively as part of a team, on a demanding project.

After two weeks, Jeanette was at the end of her rope. Not only was Charles as socially inept as a block of wood, he also refused to share his scientific data with her. The atmosphere in the small lab, where they spent entire days together, became unbearable. Jeanette found it harder and harder to sleep, and her work began to suffer. She broke out in pimples, although she'd never had acne in her life before. The dermatologist she consulted immediately concluded that her skin disorder was the result of stress.

Finally, after an out and out argument with Charles, Jeanette decided to get to the bottom of things. She discreetly questioned other colleagues who knew Charles, and tried to find out about his past behaviour. And each time he became negative with her, she made sure to write down the circumstances that provoked the conflict.

Her efforts were rewarded. In less than a week, Jeanette managed to come up with a composite portrait of the way Charles behaved:

- Charles had asked for a transfer shortly before being assigned to the project with Jeanette. His demand was refused, according to the head of personnel, because a transfer was equivalent to a promotion, and he didn't think Charles was ready for a promotion just yet.

- Charles had gotten his degree at a school that was much less prestigious than the one Jeanette went to. When Jeanette joined the company, word soon got around that she came from a top University. On that occasion, Charles had made some derisive comments about the arrival of a "new genius" on staff.

This information led Jeanette to conclude that Charles was disappointed by his superior's decision to refuse a transfer. On top of that, being forced to work with the "little genius" of the company threatened his self image, which had already been tarnished by the recent rejection.

Having evaluated the situation in this way, Jeanette decided that Charles' behaviour was due to circumstances, and was not a permanent part of his personality, as would be the case with a truly "difficult" person. This gave her the courage to confront the problem openly.

She had a frank talk with him, and as a way of affirming herself, made it clear that she did not intend to allow the situation to continue - that she would not be the target of his ill humour, since she was in no way responsible for its cause.

That's all it took. In a short time, Charles discovered that Jeanette was the best biologist he'd eve r met, and their work together proved extremely gratifying.

Do your own analysis

As you can see, it is essential that you analyse the situation yourself. Do what Jeanette did - write down the events that result in conflict with someone. You'll soon see a pattern or a series of behind-the-scenes circumstances that will shed light on the "difficult" situation.

B. Are you over-reacting?

There are some situations that just seem to do it every time - situations that we cannot tolerate, that drive us so far up the wall we finally explode in a burst of uncontrolled anger, to the astonishment of others who don't see the situation in the same way at all.

Concerning our relations with others, these kinds of excessive reactions produce feelings of immediate dislike for someone, make us get irritated over trifles, or be unnecessarily rude. In our mind, it's the other person, or persons, who are being "difficult." How do we appear to them?

You've probably noticed that when you develop an antipathy for someone, their slightest word or gesture becomes irritating. If you have this tendency, then you'd better be honest enough to admit it.

Instead of insisting that other people be less "difficult" with you, try to be a little easier on them!

How to proceed:

- Look through your journal, or search your memory for relationships of this kind that you've experienced. If you fall into this category, you won't have much trouble coming up with examples, since this type of difficult relationship is often profoundly disturbing, and not easily forgotten.

- Make a list of these people. If there's someone in your life at the moment who fits the description, use him / her as a subject for this exercise.

- Dig deep in yourself and try to find the underlying reason why you find them so hard to take. Why did you start feeling disturbed by their presence? What is it exactly that bothers you about the person? His / her attitude? Lifestyle? Voice? Personality? Way of dressing? Laughing?

- This done, try to recall your own reactions, and exactly what set them off. Write everything that comes to mind down on paper.

This kind of analysis will help you evaluate whether you're overreacting, or whether your reaction is justified.

C. Will a frank discussion be enough to clear up the situation?

This is the third question Jeanette asked herself, once she discovered the underlying causes behind Charles' negative behaviour, and was able to identify her own role in the situation.

If you find yourself facing a person who, like Charles, has been embittered by the vicissitudes of life - personal disappointments, frustrated ambitions, professional conflicts, etc. - it is possible to overcome the barrier between you without damaging either the other person or yourself, and at the same time assert yourself to advantage.

Here's what to do:

- Ask for a meeting with the other person. If necessary, set a definite time and place. Try to make sure you won't be interrupted, and show the other person that you take the problem seriously.

- Start the discussion by stating that you believe the situation between you isn't clear. Something's definitely wrong.

- Wait for the person's reaction.

- Depending on the way the person reacts - or doesn't react - to your overtures, determine what type of "difficult" person you're dealing with. You may want to read over the first few chapters of this book to refresh your memory.

- Be diplomatic! For example, after Jeanette set up a meeting with Charles, she didn't come right out and say, "Oh, I know all about what happened with your job transfer, and about your insecurity because you didn't go to a great school!"

Above all, don't be condescending or arrogant. And finally, something we can't seem to repeat often enough - DON'T TRY TO

READ THE OTHER PERSON'S MIND. There's nothing more exasperating. How would you feel if someone was constantly doing it to you?

Example:

Here's how Jeanette got the conversation rolling:

"I feel there's some tension between us, and it's beginning to affect our work. I don't have as much experience as you do, and I was hoping to learn, a lot and improve my methods by working with you. But that's not happening. Do you think we're just incompatible? Is it the mistakes I've made that are bothering you? Is it the methods I use? I'd like to know what you think about it."

2. Stop trying to change other people

This is probably one of the most important keys to success in the area of human relations. We seem to possess an extraordinary capacity for creating illusions about the people around us, and especially about those we love. We often love people despite their faults, but only because we hope that someday they'll change and conform more closely to our desired image of them.

We spend years trying to get someone to change the way we want them to, until the day comes when we realise that changing another person is beyond our powers, especially if the change we are striving to produce runs counter to that person's own will.

When that day comes, we either start loving the person for who s/he is, or we stop loving them altogether - and that's where the danger lies.

Human beings can change

This is not to deny that people have the capacity to change.

It is evident that every human being evolves throughout the course of his / her existence. The environment causes us to change, as does the exercise of individual will, and this continues right up to very old age.

But it is during the first twelve years of life that people are most malleable. And yet, even during this first phase of existence, we have the utmost difficulty getting our children to conform to our wishes.

It goes without saying that once a person reaches adulthood, his / her evolution is almost completely beyond the conscious control of anyone else, under normal circumstances.

Try to remember the last time you had an unpleasant or painful encounter with someone, and said to yourself, "If only he were less uptight!" or "If only he were a little more tolerant…" or "If only old people were less demanding…" or "If only my kids were less selfish…" and so on.

Our wishes are not reality

Our error consists of believing that others should conform to our desires, and when they don't live up to our expectations, we blame them for it. We label them difficult or intolerant, selfish or overly demanding, indecisive or vain, etc.

The important thing is to realise that we're dealing with a real human being, and that every person has his/her qualities and faults. Other people are not projections of our imagination - we can't eliminate aspects of their personality that do not live up to our expectations, nor can we give them qualities we think they should possess.

That's why I'm so pleased whenever someone says, "You're disappointing me." To me, this means that the person hasn't been in touch with who I really am, but with a projection of who they think I am - in other words, with themselves. Imagine all the time we waste being a screen for other people's projections!

So the intelligent thing to do is obviously to become conscious of the reality of people around us, both of those who please us, and those who don't. We should also know that we can contribute significantly to their happiness and self fulfilment, on condition that they wish us to do so.

You can influence people's attitudes

While you may do your utmost to improve a situation between yourself and a "difficult" person, you should under no circumstances attempt to modify that person's personality. You will not succeed, and in any case it won't be of any use.

The only thing you can do is modify a person's attitude toward you. It is towards this goal that you should direct all your efforts.

You do more for the person this way than by trying to change his / her personality, and make the person easier to live with, from your point of view, of course.

By bringing the problem or conflict that is poisoning your relationship out in the open, you help the other person see him / herself more clearly, just as you've been able to see yourself better because of the efforts you've been making.

And it is by becoming aware of the forces, the ambitions, the desires and repulsions that make us act in certain ways, that enable us to take control of our lives, assert ourselves and attain fulfilment.

3. Distance yourself

As we'll see in more detail in Chapter 7, it is indispensable to learn how to protect yourself from the damage difficult people and conflict situations can cause.

When faced with a difficult relationship, we tend to get deeply involved. We lose all sense of objectivity. Our day to day lives are soon affected, as we become preoccupied with the problem. We may even become obsessed by the difficult person in question, and the problems s/he is causing.

This is what happened at first to Jeaneatte, our biologist. Overwhelmed by her problems with Charles, she became unable to sleep, couldn't do her work properly, until she took hold of herself and analysed the situation as if she were an outside observer.

But keeping your distance from someone who exerts a strong influence is easier said than done. Difficult people seem to know how to trigger negative emotions - they always seem to know just what to say or do to make us upset.

That's why we've dedicated an entire chapter to the techniques that help protect you, and allow you to remain detached.

4. Adopt a strategy and apply it

In your exchanges with difficult people, there are really only two types of strategy to choose from. Either you get involved in a power struggle, with the aim of coming out on top. Or you look for a way to achieve satisfying results while taking the other person's needs into account.

The upper hand

As we've seen in previous chapters, there are different types of "difficult" people, so it follows that our strategy will depend on the type of attack that you are subjected to.

For example, if you're dealing with a negative type, who gradually manages to intoxicate your mind with measured doses of pessimism, you'd be less inclined to get into a power struggle situation than if you were dealing with a "steamroller" type.

When we look at the world around us, we see that the struggle for survival seems to resemble a frantic competition, where the big fish swallow up the little fish, and the strong dominate the weak. So there's a great temptation to consider our relations with difficult people as a struggle, where the only aim is to gain the upper hand.

However, you've probably noticed that in the preceding chapters we have avoided suggesting that gaining the upper hand become the main objective of your training in interpers on al relations.

Avoid win - lose situations

The reason for this approach is that wherever you have a win - lose situation, the loser will not rest until s/he has found some way of getting revenge. We could even qualify this reaction as "natural" since it is so common.

But if you think about it, you'll see that although the animal kingdom does rely on the balance created by the strong devouring the weak, nowhere in nature do we see a weak animal waiting patiently for years, and sometimes even for generations if necessary, in order to reverse the roles and exact revenge on another animal, for a past humiliation.

This is a characteristically human trait, which, as we know, results in all kinds of disasters - wars, famine, repression, needless destruction, and so on.

This is why our recommendations are aimed at "restoring communication at the point where it broke down" and "defining your position, as well as that of the other person, if necessary." Not letting someone walk all over you doesn't necessarily mean dominating that person. It means not letting another person dominate you and, based on this affirmation of self, doing something constructive about the situation.

Win-win strategy and the game of life

Another way to approach our relations with others is to try to produce a situation that satisfies both our needs, as well as the other person's.

In Chapter 5, we analysed the process whereby a person accumulates negative points against someone else. We score more negative points each time we come out a loser in a relationship. When we win, we score positive points.

There are people for whom we feel no special sympathy, who surprise us with the generous and unsolicited things they do for us. Each time we feel like a winner in our relations with them, we are, consciously or unconsciously, scoring a golden point in their favour. The day may come when they do something that tips the scales, this time in a positive sense, and we find ourselves experiencing an immense feeling of gratitude towards them.

A narrow view of life could give us the impression that nature is nothing more than a huge battlefield. But science has shown us that, above all, nature is a study in balance. If a species disappears because of a predator's success, the predator will also disappear, for lack of food.

The more progress we make in understanding the universe, the more we discover that everything is somehow related to everything else. Winning by forcing someone else to lose out ultimately means setting yourself up to lose out as well. That's the way the game of life works. We're all in the same boat, and if I make a hole in the hull because I want you to sink, I'm eventually going to sink too.

In fact, what is occurring now, thanks to developments in science and communication, is a mutation of consciousness which is unprecedented in the history of humanity. We are discovering that the choice of being a winner by making others losers, is not a real choice at all. The real choice is that either we both win together, or we both lose together. This is the only alternative we have. And that's why we must develop a win - win attitude, to the point where it becomes a reflex, in almost all situations.

When we're dealing with likable, nice, easy-going people, it happens naturally. We find certain people "disarming" and couldn't imagine doing anything to harm them, probably because we'd feel too guilty afterwards.

On the other hand, when we have to deal with difficult persons, things become a lot harder, probably because we feel they have wronged us in some way, and we wish to punish them for it.

We have the choice

However, even in these types of situations we have the choice of creating a relationship based on force and domination, a relationship which is bound to fail eventually, or to look for a way to satisfy both parties.

We are never obliged to use force. If you think differently, go back and read Chapter 3 which deals with the issue of individual responsibility, and the way we unconsciously encourage victim oriented situations, which usually end tragically, to develop.

When faced with a difficult person, you have to be very clear on what strategy you intend using: are you going to try and crush the other person in order to experience the pleasure (albeit very temporary) of victory or revenge, without thinking about the price you'll have to pay later for your elation?

Or are you going to protect yourself first, and then look for ways to establish a constructive dialogue?

These two fundamental options are always available to you. The only variable, therefore, is your choice of approach.

Become aware of negative interaction

The main problem with applying a win - win approach is that the negativity which characterises the communication can easily engender more negativity in you. This is what is meant by negative interaction - the old vicious circle.

They're sometimes impossible to avoid. We're so upset and exasperated that any possibility of improving the situation, or bringing it to a positive conclusion, seems very remote.

When you're the target of anger, slander, and injustice, it can be all but impossible to control yourself, and not react in kind.

However, if you wish to assert yourself, improve the situation, and help the other person all at the same time, then you have no choice. You must learn to control the way you react, in order to break the vicious circle and set up a cycle of positive interaction in its place.

What you're being asked to do, in order to defuse conflict situations and start communicating with difficult persons, is to respond to their anger with patience, to their disdain with respect, and to their harmful intentions with benevolence.

If you think that this is a superhuman task, reserved for angels and saints, then you will inevitably perpetuate the cycles of misunderstanding and violence you encounter. But rest assured, although reacting in this way may be reserved for "evolved" persons, it is by no means beyond the reach of the average human being.

The simple fact that you've read this far is sufficient proof that developing such reflexes would not present much of a problem for you. All you have to do is practice the exercises suggested a little later on.

Above all, strive for positive interaction

Here's some good news: in the same way that negative attracts negative, positive attracts positive. The hard thing to do is reverse the current, and we'll be looking here at a few methods for effecting this change.

We've already stressed the importance of not responding to aggression with aggression. We must refer to it again, since it is the cornerstone of achieving any significant changes in your conflicting or difficult relationships.

We analysed how difficult persons seem to have the capacity for bringing out the worst in us, for bringing us down to their level, so that we find ourselves doing the very same things we've been criticising them for doing! However, don't forget that as difficult as a person may be, s/he is still capable of responding positively to the right kind of stimulus; everyone (almost) possesses all the necessary resources for becoming an open, positive and communicative person.

To start the process, you must first categorically refuse to participate in any destructive games. Then, when attempts to involve you in such games cease, you can start your work being the engine that pulls the relationship in a positive direction.

Get rid of all the garbage and junk that is weighing you down. Start collecting "golden points" in all your relationships. Create conditions for positive interaction, for "virtuous" circles instead of vicious ones. I guarantee your life will undergo a miraculous change for the better.

Conditions for the success of your strategy

All right, say you're ready to play "win - win" communication with your steamroller boss, your incisive colleague, your whining spouse, and your neighbour the clam. Whatever they say or do, you won't let it get to you. You'll stay floating up there on your cloud of objectivity, sending back positive messages. You're in the perfect frame of mind. Be firm, and you'll succeed.

But please, don't make your task more difficult than it already is, by choosing the wrong moment.

Make sure your subject is not under any excess pressure

You've finished reading this book. You've done all your preparation exercises, and you feel better armed than ever to put an end to some negative interaction which has been poisoning your existence.

You've summoned all your courage, and decided that the big confrontation is to take place next Monday, after work.

What you're about to do may have an extremely positive impact on the person concerned. However, experience has shown that people are much more open to criticism when they are given some solid data to relate that criticism to.

As far as you can judge, make sure your "target" is not especially vulnerable at the moment, because of any undue stress caused by overwork, illness, serious personal problems, etc.

If you don't, you risk upsetting the delicate balance the person is trying to maintain, in order to get through a difficult time. You will meet with much more resistance than at other moments, and your attempt will probably fail.

I've known people who were completely unreceptive to any suggestion of change, simply because they were going through a tough time in their lives, and had absolutely no desire to make any extra effort. However, after the crisis passed, these same people showed themselves to be very ready to evolve.

There are two lessons to be learned from this: first, you can't force things. Next, don't get discouraged because you don't succeed on your first attempt. It may just be an indication that, for the person in question, the time is not right.

You shouldn't be under any excess pressure either

In order to bring your operation to a successful conclusion, you will have to draw on all your resources of patience, understanding and adaptation. To do this, you must be in top shape. Any vulnerability on your part can result in failure.

Maybe you think this is obvious. Well, you'd be surprised at how frequently we show signs of being under excessive pressure without even knowing about it. The signs are much easier to detect in others...

Therefore, make sure you analyse your own situation first. If you've undergone some serious trauma in the last few months (radical change of lifestyle, death of someone close to you, accident, marriage, divorce, a move, a promotion or loss of job, important exams, etc.) wait until you've regained your sense of equilibrium completely.

If you don't, you'll only be adding one more element of tension to those already upsetting your life, and your efforts will be futile. You won't have the energy to deal with the situation properly. You'll start believing you were wrong to try and change anything in the first place, and that you're incapable of succeeding. All this simply because the time may not be right! First take care of yourself, then deal with others...

Prepare a worst-case scenario

This is a good precaution to take before confronting difficult persons: think about what you will do if none of your efforts result in any improvement in the relationship.

Ask yourself what the worst possible consequence would be if you did not make any attempt to rectify the situation. If you continue doing what you've been doing all along, what would happen?

Write this down in your notebook - you'll refer to it later when you evaluate the effectiveness of your actions. This is what you hope to avoid by resorting to the measures described here, in this book. Any result that is likely to be better than your worst-case scenario, can be qualified as a success.

Now ask yourself what other solutions might work in case your first attempt meets with failure. Perhaps you've been thinking about murdering the person, they have such an intolerable influence on you! Or you way be considering leaving the country. I hope my advice helps you avoid such extremes.

But seriously, ask yourself what you'd do if the relationship does not improve. There's nothing worse than feeling caught in a trap, especially since the trap is not a real one. We are never condemned to live, in perpetuity, with someone whom we find impossible to tolerate; or to work for or with some who makes our life a living hell. There's always at least one, and usually a number of alternatives open to us, which we must prepare for in our minds, before the fact if possible.

If you don't think you have any alternatives, you'll always find yourself with your back to the wall. The very fact that you're so anxious to get results will seriously reduce your chances for success. On the other hand, if you have other options, you will be more objective in the face of an initial failure, and at the same time much more effective.

You may ultimately decide, after thinking things over, that leaving things be is preferable to making another attempt at reconciliation.

If so, you have every right to withdraw, and leave the difficult person to his / her own devices.

Evaluate the pro's and con's carefully

The pro's and con's must be evaluated carefully before taking any action. You should be aware of the risks you're taking, the dangers involved, and the possible consequences.

Once you've done this, forget about your doubts, and concentrate all your efforts on the positive effects you wish to produce. Remember that the difference between winners and losers is that losers think about what they're afraid will happen, while winners think about what they want to happen.

CHAPTER 7
The Weapon of Words:

Putting Them To Good Use

Words are weapons. They can cut as deeply as a knife blade. The scars they leave are perhaps less visible, but they are just as painful.

A child would prefer to be spanked rather than ridiculed by his / her peers for being a tattletale or teacher's pet.

What better proof of the power of words than the fact that the more a political regime is repressive, the more it prohibits freedom of speech. Freedom of speech is the first civil right to be guaranteed by a democracy, and suppressed by a dictatorship. And abuse of language (in the form of libel, slander, mental cruelty etc.) even in democracies, is prohibited by law.

But in personal communication, such control is not possible. Every day, millions of people are submitted to some kind of verbal abuse. It may be in the form of a more or less subtle insult, a cutting remark, a complaint, a forced silence - whatever form the abuse takes, it still hurts.

On the other hand, words are also instruments of healing and pleasure. They can be used to calm someone who is being aggressive, to carry on a dialogue instead of a fight, and to negotiate.

In the previous chapters, we've been looking at ways to defend yourself against attacks while remaining calm and in control.

The time has come to round off some of the techniques you've been exposed to, to help you avoid abusing the weapon of words, and to pave the way for fruitful negotiations that will resolve potentially explosive situations.

The three commandments of defence

Using the weapon of words to defend yourself requires an understanding and mastery of three basic principles.

1. Know how to recognise an attack

Some attacks are obvious. Others may seem like attacks, but aren't. Still others may not seem like attacks, but are.

When an angry driver jumps out of his car with his fist raised and rushes towards you screaming, "Bloody idiot! I'm going to shove this through your face!", you can be pretty sure you're dealing with a verbal attack, which will probably soon turn into a physical one.

But under other circumstances, we may think we are being attacked when we aren't. As you know, some people are short-tempered and easily offended, even though they may have the best intentions in the world. If you are one of these people, take care not to see harm where, in fact, there is none.

Finally, some attacks are so well disguised they don't appear to be attacks at all. This may seem unimportant if we consider that an attack only becomes troublesome when it affects us, and that if we don't notice it, it can't be affecting us! But there's a Chinese proverb which says: "Water droplets can do more harm than a violent storm, because they eventually split the hardest rock, while the storm leaves it intact."

So there are verbal attacks which we may not recognise, either because they're well disguised and very subtle, or because they come from persons with whom we think we have a positive relationship.

An example:

Mary has a nineteen year old daughter, Louise. She's a pleasant, good natured adolescent, with a kind heart and a winning smile.

Then, on a few occasions, Mary noticed that Louise came home in a bad mood. She seemed troubled, and on the point of breaking into tears at the slightest provocation.

After further observation, Mary was able to relate Louise's mood shifts to the times she went out with her best friend, Carol. But when questioned, Louise insisted she and Carol were still best of friends.

Mary determined to investigate further, and try to get to the bottom of things. She observed Carol whenever she came over to the house to visit Louise, and soon realised that her daughter was being victimised by Carol, without being aware of it.

During their conversations, which appeared outwardly friendly, Carol constantly kept pricking Louise with sharp little verbal attacks, so subtle as to be almost imperceptible. Louise had no idea that she was the target of a constant flow of verbal abuse.

For example, Louise was a little self conscious about being thin, but it didn't bother her until Carol calmly announced that... "I bought my dress for the graduation party. It's really low cut. Of course, not everyone can wear that kind of dress." This particular thorn was aimed directly at Louise's rather bony clavicles.

In this way, Louise was being gradually poisoned by her relationship with Carol, without knowing it. And this is what lay behind her apparently inexplicable mood changes, which would occur after she spent time with Carol.

This type of attack falls into the "cutting remark" category. While it is more subtle, and therefore harder to detect, it is just as harmful.

The lesson gained from this example is that you must, at all cost, protect yourself against toxic persons and refuse to make them part of your circle of friends and acquaintances. Either you let them know that they will have to change their behaviour if they want to maintain a relationship with you, or you distance yourself from them right away.

2. Adapt your defence to the kind of attack

You have to adapt your defence strategy to the type of attack being levelled at you, not only in terms of quality, but also intensity.

It would be useless to expend a lot of energy reducing an unskilled adversary to tears. In the first place it would be cowardly, and in the second place, your aim is not to destroy someone but to respond in a way that will eventually help.

If you intend to pave the way for a dialogue in order to get something from the other person later on, then running that person into the ground will hardly be in your best interests. On the contrary, you want to deal with someone who respects you, because you have skillfully and diplomatically remedied a difficult situation.

We are all capable of affirming ourselves without crushing other people. Unfortunately, too many people refuse to understand this simple principle.

"If you really loved me, you wouldn't be such a spendthrift," a husband tells his wife.

The woman could make use of one of the techniques you read about earlier, by saying something like, "Isn't it interesting that so many men are under the impression - totally unjustified, of course - that their wives don't love them..."

The confrontation could, and should end there. The husband will no doubt be surprised by his wife's objective reaction, and he'll probably change the subject as soon as possible.

However, the wife could have responded quite differently: "It's really interesting that a lot of men, once they've reached your age, start thinking that their wives don't love them any more." With that little dig, she gets her revenge.

But be careful. If you give in to this type of temptation, you can expect the argument to continue as soon as the other person has collected him/herself, and you should make sure that you are sufficiently armed to counter any subsequent attacks.

If you're dealing with someone close to you, then this type of counter attack will probably lead to a session of verbal ping pong, which as you now know can be very dangerous. It's much better to avoid this kind of petty vengeance, no matter how skillful you are at verbal duelling, because sooner or later you'll pay the price.

3. Carry your defence strategy through to the end

Defending yourself against a difficult person may require being hard and incisive. If you're not used to acting this way, you may start feeling guilty, become indecisive, and cut your efforts short half way through.

Contrary to what you may think, few people are adept at being verbally tough. It's always the same people who brutalise others, and their skill doesn't depend on age or size: some extremely dangerous steamroller types are still in grade school!

Consider verbal self-defence as a kind of martial art. As such, it is not an incitement to violence. On the contrary, its aim is to put an end to the violence that is being perpetrated against you. It allows you to affirm yourself and get what you want without having to resort to force. So don't stop half way through, and don't allow your surprise to paralyse you. Be firm and energetic! A red hot iron, although painful, can prevent a wound from becoming infected and destroying an entire body.

Attack: the most frequent types

In Chapters 2, 3, 4 and 5, we presented a few examples of different kinds of attacks launched by "difficult" persons you are likely to encounter.

In this chapter, we offer more examples, classified according to the precise type of attack they represent. Use them to plan and prepare your counter measures.

First, let's look at the two main types of "subtle" attack:

- disguised accusations
- emotional blackmail

1. Disguised accusations

Disguised accusations are the easiest kind of verbal attack to disarm, as long as you're able to stay cool. There are are number of types. Here are the most common. With a little practice, you'll be able to recognise them immediately.

Type A: "If you really…"

a. An adolescent to his/her parents: "If you really want me to do well in school, you'd buy me a computer…"

b. A spouse to his / her partner: "If you really loved me, you wouldn't talk to me like that…"

c. A teacher to a student: "If you really wanted to get your diploma, you wouldn't skip every second class…"

d. A doctor to a patient: "If you really wanted to lose weight, you wouldn't eat so many sweets…"

Each of these disguised accusations implies something:

a. You don't care whether I do well in school or not... therefore you are bad parents.

b. You don't love me because you don't show any consideration for me.

c. You don't want to graduate.

d. Either you don't care about your weight, or you haven't got enough willpower to stop eating sweets.

A variation of this type of disguised aggression, which uses an impersonal accusation, is slightly more subtle, but its effect is the same:

a. "Parents who care about their children wouldn't think twice about buying a computer, if it could help with their schoolwork..."

b. "When you love someone, you don't use that tone of voice..."

c. "A student who wants to graduate doesn't skip every second class..."

d. "A person who really wants to lose weight doesn't stuff themselves with sweets..."

Type B: Even... should...

e. A good skier to a beginner: "Even a beginner should be able to take this hill..."

f. A patient to his / her nurse: "Even a simple nurse should realise when someone is suffering..." And finally, two remarks that really hit below the belt, but which, unfortunately, husbands and children are expert at using:

g. A child to his / her mother:

The Weapon of Words "Mother, even you should be able to understand that I need some new summer clothes..." h. A husband to his wife: "Even you should be able to learn how to drive a car properly..." This type of disguised accusation is more lethal than the first. It implies much more than it seems to say, and in fact represents a series of attacks, one on top of another.

If we decode the messages we find:

- e. Beginner skiers aren't very smart. You don't have to be a good skier to go down this hill. If you can't, it's because you're totally inept.

- f. You don't have to be smart to be a nurse, but you're even less intelligent than other nurses if you can't tell when a patient is suffering.

In other words: You may be a complete imbecile, but there are still some things you should be able to understand (or do).

Obviously the attacker is perfectly aware of what s/he's doing. The intention is to cause you harm, to make you react in a negative way, to show his / her superiority, and to place you in a no-win situation. This is the moment to remember the 3 golden rules for defending yourself against attack:

- Don't respond to aggressiveness by being aggressive;
- Take time to think and breathe deeply;
- Throw the aggressor off guard by not getting upset.

Practical training

Now try to come up with at least one response (comprised of one or two possible replies) for each accusation of this type.

The only way to master the weapon of words is to practice defending yourself in situations where someone is playing a win-lose type of game with you.

At the end of this book, you'll find an "Annex to Chapter 7" with suggested responses to all these situations.

Example of Type A response: "If you really…"

   a. An adolescent to his / her parents:

"If you really wanted me to do well in school, you'd buy me a computer…"

Parent: "Now now, when did you start thinking I didn't want you to do well in school?"

Comment: Note the literal interpretation of the child's statement. The parent expressly ignores the second part of the statement.

Child: "Because you won't buy me a computer! All my friends have one…"

Comment: The child is forced to show his / her hand. S/he is forced to admit the s/he wants a computer because all the other kids have one.

Parent: "Alright, but can you tell me how a computer is going to help you get your diploma and do better in school? For example, how are you going to use a computer during your exams?"

Comment: Once again the parent takes what the child says completely seriously, and forces the child to offer more explanations. The child can no longer complain that the parent doesn't care if s/he does well or not. In this way, the disguised blackmail has been easily neutralised.

Now it's your turn:

- b. Spouse A to Spouse B: "If you really loved me, you wouldn't talk to me like that..."

- Response by spouse B:

- Spouse A:

- Spouse B:

- c. A professor to a student: "If you really wanted to graduate, my friend, you wouldn't skip every second class..."

- Student:

- Professor:

- Student:

d. A doctor to a patient: "If you really wanted to lose weight, you wouldn't eat so many sweets..."

- Patient:

- Doctor:

- Patient:

Example of Type B: Even... should...

e. Expert skier to a beginner: "Even you should be able to get down this hill..."

Beginner: "Oh that makes me feel a whole lot better! You mean even someone totally inept like me is capable of getting down here?"

Comment: The beginner at first seems to be calmly repeating what the expert said. S/he then shows that s/he is fully aware of the expert's condescending tone.

Expert: "No no, that's not what I meant..."

Comment: The expert could have tried to get out of it by saying something like, "No, you misunderstood me. All I was trying to say is that this is a very easy hill." But the surprise effect worked, and s/he was at a momentary loss for words.

Beginner: "It's okay, a lot of people are like that. Once they get good at something, they think anyone who can't do it is just stupid. But I didn't expect that kind of thing from you."

Comment: One of the best ways to respond to this type of accusation is to shift the issue to an impersonal level.

Your turn again:

- f. Patient to nurse:
  "Even a nurse should understand when someone is suffering..."

- Nurse:

- Patient:

- Nurse:

- g. Child to mother:
  "Mother, even you should realise that I need some new summer clothes..."

- Mother:

- Child:

- Mother:

- h. Husband to wife:
  "Even you, my dear, should be able to learn how to drive a car properly..."

- Wife:

- Husband:

- Wife:

2. Appealing to emotions

At first glance, this type of verbal attack is not as harmful as disguised accusations. Nevertheless, they are embarrassing, and often exasperating, sometimes enough to make you respond with aggression.

Form whom should you expect this kind of attack? In general, from persons who are close to you, and who know what your weak points are. They know what you've made of your life, and what your complexes, fears and ambitions are.

If you want to maintain the relationship, don't counter attack! Simply defend yourself. Once again, the same rules apply:

- Don't respond to aggressiveness by being aggressive; - Take time to think and breathe deeply;
- Throw the aggressor off guard by not getting upset.

You can easily recognise an appeal to emotion because this type of attack always starts in the same way. Here are a few illustrations, which you'll refer to later in your practical training:

Examples

  i. An adolescent to his / her mother: "Why don't you ever try to be nice to me?"

j. A husband to his wife: "Why do you always try to make me look like an idiot?"

k. A parent to a child: "Can't you ever try to please me?"

The phrases "Why... never" and "Can't you...ever" simply mean "You never..." and constitute an admonishment, an accusation, and an appeal for pity all at the same time.

It would be tempting to reply with something like:

i. "How dare you say that I'm never nice to you! After all I've done for you..."

j. "You think I make you look stupid? Well my dear, you do very well on your own, without any help from me!"

k. "I know, I know. You regret ever having me. What do you want me to do? I didn't ask to be born!"

Since this type of attack is common in close relationships, it can quickly develop into the kind of verbal ping pong situation we looked at in Chapter 5.

Practical training

Here are illustrations of correct responses to these three examples:

i. An adolescent to his / her mother:

"Why don't you ever try to be nice to me?"

Mother's response: "Well now, what could I do that you think would be nice? Would you like me to stay home and wait for you to come home from your football games or your parties? Let's sit down in the den, and I'll make you a nice cup of hot chocolate. You can tell me all about the game, and the party. We could have a real talk. Would you like that?"

Comment: The mother neutralises the situation in two ways. Firstly, by doing exactly what the child wants her to do (being nice) she gives him / her the attention s/he is demanding. Secondly, what the mother suggests (hot chocolate and a chat) is not likely to excite the child a whole lot: these days, the last thing an adolescent wants is to have his / her mother waiting at home to hear all about the day's events!

Child: "What do you mean! That's a stupid idea..."

Mother: "Oh. Well, let's not talk any more about it then. It was just an idea. If you don't like it, we'll find something else to do..."

Comment: The mother comes out with flying colours. She makes no blunders, and meets with no resistance. She demonstrates her good intentions, and at the same time achieves her goals. No one gets hurt and the problem is resolved peacefully.

Your turn:

j. A husband to his wife:

"Why do you always try to make me look like an idiot?"

- Wife:
- Husband:
- Wife:

k. A parent to a child: "Can't you ever try to please me?"
Child: Parent: Child:

Words as weapons: Conclusions

As you've seen, most verbal attacks are provocations, which also contain various negative implications. Consciously or not, the attacker expects you to react in a certain way.

What allows you to save the situation is the element of surprise. You can come out a winner, with neither side losing out, if you can react in a way that doesn't fit the pattern, and for which the attacker has had no time to elaborate a response.

It's impossible to predict all the situations in which you may become the object of disguised verbal attacks. The examples in this chapter represent the most common variations. But with a little practice, you will be able to recognise disguised attacks as they occur, even if they appear in an unusual form.

In any case, rest assured that whatever form the attack takes, and

The Weapon of Words whatever your response is, you can remain in control of the situation if you manage to take the aggressor by surprise. And in the final analysis, being master of the situation is what counts! (See the Appendix at the end of the book for more suggestions on how to respond to the illustrations in this chapter.)

CHAPTER 8
Shields and Inner Strength

In our relations with others, we meet people who are sources of comfort, inspiration and hope. These people constitute a blessing, when permitted to make their contributions to our lives.

However, there are also people who provoke disagreement, anger and discouragement, the so-called "difficult" types. In our relations with them, we experience apprehension, frustration, and even suffering.

Throughout this book, we have suggested exercises and methods to help you open a line of communication with these people, imprisoned as they are in a shell of silence, or behind a wall of venomous barbs. To make this kind of approach possible, you need to protect yourself against the wounds that may be inflicted, and develop your inner strength.

How to recognise the different levels of aggression

When someone uses language as a weapon against you, which part of you is hurt?

Shields and Inner Strength Why does it hurt when someone opposes you in obstinate silence, or seems to see right through you? When you are insulted, why do you suffer? Answering these questions will enable you to recognise the signs of verbal attack. But you also have to learn to distinguish between the different levels of aggression directed at you.

Shows of physical aggression

On a physical level, there are a number of elements which we use as references, and which form parts of our overall communication. These elements are images, sounds, and tactile impressions. When we see "difficult" persons in action, we may be impressed by their absurd, exaggerated gestures, or intimidated by the volume of their shouting, or even bodily harmed if they attack us physically.

If you're sensitive to sound, and you know you have to attend a meeting where a difficult colleague, whose voice is always grating and much too loud, is going to speak, get yourself a pair of earplugs at the pharmacy and use them! At least the noise will be sufficiently muffled so you can remain comfortable, no matter how loud your difficult colleague becomes.

It is possible to learn how to remain impassive while someone is standing right in front of you and insulting you. This is part of an American G.I.'s training. But plugging your ears works just as well, and requires a lot less practice.

As far as images are concerned, if you're fortunate enough to be short-sighted, remove your glasses! Let the person make all the terrible faces s/he wants. If you're unlucky and have 20/20 vision, look at something else - the person's shoes, for example - they're harmless enough. Don't look at the hands - they can be quite frightening. If this doesn't work, you can resort to humour, which we'll be looking at in the last chapter. When confronted with a terrifying image, humour is one of the best ways of transforming it into a harmless and amusing caricature.

Stay far enough away...

Finally, there is physical aggression proper. You may be physically attacked. Always remember that it takes two to fight, and that it is very unlikely that someone will attack you physically if you do absolutely nothing to provoke it. Simply remaining firm and impassive in the face of aggression will not encourage a person to strike you, unless s/he is deranged. Be sure to maintain sufficient physical distance between yourself and the potential aggressor, so as not to be taken by surprise. And if you've studied a little martial arts, all the better...

You should be aware that all aggression is accompanied by a more or less powerful discharge of negative energy, depending on who you're dealing with. You can feel this discharge right in the pit of your stomach. You will notice that an offending remark or threat does not hurt in your brain, or in your heart, or in your knees. You feel it in a region just below the solar plexus, i.e. right in the gut.

According to Hindu tradition, this area of the body contains a centre which can perceive discharges of negative energy directly. This explains why we cross our arms when we feel threatened. Our arms form a physical barrier between the source of aggression and the centre in us, which is sensitive to this kind of energy. The same protection can be obtained by holding a book or a purse in front of your stomach.

Shows of intellectual aggression

You'll also become the object of intellectual attacks in your encounters with difficult people. They may ridicule your ideas, or argue with you in a very intelligent way in order to put you at fault. Others will always be able to pinpoint the reason or the exception that proves you're wrong, at least about the subject in question. Others are expert at bluffing, still others at twisting your words...

To deal with these kinds of threats, you practically have to be a master of rhetoric, and keep your mind fluid and clear. For centuries, rhetoric was taught in schools as a separate and important discipline, right up to the university level. Today, rhetoric has been dropped from most schools' curriculum, and we all have to improvise as best we can in order to defend ourselves.

If you are worried about not measuring up on an intellectual level against someone, then don't get involved in discussions that will leave you vulnerable and exposed to attack. Let the other person demonstrate his / her erudition, and listen, or at least make a show of listening, attentively to what they say. When they've finished, ask if they have anything to add to what they've already said. When they have exhausted their opinions, all you have to say is something like, "Well, from your point of view, you are certainly correct..." implying that you hold a different point of view. Then you carry on with whatever you were saying before the attack, as if nothing happened.

Or you can say that you didn't understand the argument, which places the aggressor in the difficult position of having to explain his / her point of view all over again (with no guarantee of being understood this time either!) or of just letting it drop.

Persons who practice this type of aggression find it very annoying to have to repeat themselves, because they usually come out looking a lot worse the second time around.

Shows of emotional aggression are both physical and mental

We are most vulnerable on the emotional level. We often feel drained after an encounter with a difficult person, and it's obvious that one essential condition for the success of the techniques we've been suggesting is that you are able to remain calm during an attack.

However, it is very hard to neutralise a negative emotion that is affecting us with another, opposing emotion which could act as an antidote. Emotions affect our entire organism, and provoke neuro- chemical reactions in us which take take time to complete.

That's why it is imperative to practice using mental exercises and techniques that can help you control your emotions. You can prepare yourself against the potentially devastating effects of emotion. To do this, you resort to "shields" and to exercises designed to develop your inner strength.

The paradox about protecting ourselves against emotional suffering is that we've been doing it since childhood. The result is that by the time we become adults, many of us have completely suppressed our emotional reactions, to the point where nothing seems to affect us. The anaesthesia we've been administering to ourselves since infancy has become so generalised that we cannot be hurt emotionally. The downside to this is that we anaesthetise ourselves against positive emotions as well, and find ourselves cut off from all the positive aspects of human emotion, such as love and affection.

Shields and Inner Strength The recommendations in this chapter are not meant to help emotionally deprived persons, who should first seek help and try to establish some balance in their emotional lives.

Other people seem momentarily upset when subjected to emotional attack, but quickly regain their composure, like a professional boxer who bounces back after a particularly punishing blow. This is the best way to behave when dealing with difficult people: neither too insensitive, nor too vulnerable. The advice in this chapter is meant to reinforce this state.

Finally, there are people who are extremely sensitive. Emotional blows leave scars which take a long time to heal. Even the thought of facing a "difficult" person gives them the butterflies, and yet somewhere, they find the courage to do so. It is for these people especially that I wrote this chapter.

Why do we suffer?

When sensitive persons become the object of emotional attacks, what is it that makes them suffer? All the research and analysis points to the same thing: people suffer because their self image - or self esteem, which is more or less the same thing - is threatened.

Starting in childhood, we build our personality around a central core, which is the image we have of ourselves. The more this image is solid and positive, the more unlikely we are to have emotional problems. The more self esteem we have, the harder it is for us to believe that others do not hold us in very high esteem as well, and therefore the harder it is for us to suffer.

Who better than ourselves can provide the esteem and love we need to overcome all the problems of life? However, this supposes that we have been raised with a sufficient measure of love and encouragement throughout our childhood. Unfortunately, that often isn't the case.

If our self image is defective or fragile, we are much more vulnerable to attack. Guiding you through an in-depth programme for reaffirming your self image and self esteem is beyond the scope of this book. For one thing, it would be very difficult to do on your own, without personal counselling. However, what you can do is maintain your self image as it is, and put a series of shields into place to protect it.

Automatic suffering and how to stop it

You've surely remarked that there are certain situations, certain spoken messages or even single words, that get to you every time, and always in the same way. In the chapter on words as weapons, we showed you just how powerful language can be. We'll now take our analysis a step further to include all kinds of stimuli, including those which are non-verbal, which set off an automatic suffering response.

Deadly gestures and phrases

Have you ever worked very hard at something, only to feel that your efforts were neither understood nor appreciated? What was said or done to create this impression? Have you ever wanted to show someone something you wrote or built, some music you composed, or share an idea for a project, only to hold back for fear of being rejected and ridiculed? What was it in your past experience that made you afraid not to be appreciated?

We've all had feelings, thoughts and creative ideas that have been "killed", nullified, soiled and rejected by other people's comments, gestures and mocking attitudes. We've all been made to feel stupid, ridiculous or clumsy by our parents, our fellow students, our superiors, colleagues... and especially by the "difficult" people we encounter.

Deadly phrases

What all deadly phrases have in common is that they attack our self esteem, sometimes seriously, to the point where psychologists have labelled them "deadly."

When we expose ourselves by revealing some hidden treasure, we are not always sure of its relative worth. Is the song or poem I wrote any good? Do I dare show it to someone, or should I keep it to myself, in case the person doesn't like it, and says something that makes me feel completely worthless...

Some of the most frequently used deadly phrases are:

"I haven't got time now... (to a child who's all excited and wants to show you a drawing...)

"That's a stupid idea... you know it's impossible!" (to an adolescent who's told you about a project to cycle around the world...)

"Are you serious? You'll never make it! And anyway, it's already been done. It's a ludicrous thing even to consider. You've got the mind of a child ..." and so on.

On-off switches

Different individuals are sensitive to different words and gestures. What may totally demolish your neighbour may leave you cold as stone. What hurts you may hurt only you, and no one else. This is due to the process which associates words and emotions. There are words which immediately provoke a pleasant sensation in us. Others makes us deeply uncomfortable, without our knowing why.

To understand this process better, think about the insults and other phrases which disturb you the most. They could have something to do with being lazy, miserly, weak, effeminate, past your prime, unreasonable, a failure, a lost cause, etc.

When you discover a word or phrase that hurts you, you will no doubt associate it with a voice, an image, or a feeling which goes way back to your past. These words and gestures have been engraved in your file of early negative experiences, and that's why you automatically react to them in such an intense way.

Let's look at the process objectively. Say you go purple with rage every time someone suggests that you're a failure. We can assume that the person saying this knows you well enough to be aware that the word will hurt you. This word is like the switch on an appliance. Someone says, "You're a failure..." and you blow your top. What has happened to your free will?

Are we puppets?

She slams the door: I get depressed. She says, "Is that it?" and I shrivel up. She says, "You're still tired?" and I get angry...

This person is walking around with a typewriter stuck to his chest - you press a certain key and... bang! You get the reaction you want... always. Are human beings robots or machines, programmed from childhood to react in a specific way?

In part, yes.

The repetition of certain behaviour engraves positive and negative experiences in our minds, and causes us to react automatically, and in the same way, to a given set of circumstances. Some people are so controlled by these habitual reactions that they seem like real live puppets - all you have to do is pull the strings.

We can change or eliminate automatic reactions

Fortunately, human beings cannot be reduced to mere automatons. We have the power to change or eliminate our habits. Some people practice doing this their whole lives, and claim to be completely liberated from their automatic reactions. However, I haven't met the person yet who can drink a salty cup of coffee without automatically making a face! Most people reside somewhere between the puppet and the completely liberated spirit. We function automatically a part of the time, and gradually gain more control over ourselves as we make progress in our efforts at self development.

How to desensitise ourselves

The "switches" that control us do so without our knowing. When my wife would slam the door as she left the apartment after a minor dispute, I felt like she'd slapped me in the face, and I would dramatise the event to an extreme. I finally realised that this switch was very harmful, since it provoked me into continuing the dispute, when what I really wanted was to calm things down.

However, despite the fact that I became aware of my automatic reaction, each time my wife slammed the door, I fell into the trap. I would jump up, my heart racing, and shout curses after her. By the time I realised that I'd reacted automatically again, it was too late - the damage was done.

This went on until I had the bright idea of asking my wife to repeat the gesture, as many times as was required for me to neutralise my automatic reaction. She slammed the door once, then a second and third time... After some minutes, I was able to remain totally impassive when she slammed the door shut, and it hasn't bothered me since.

How to neutralise deadly phrases

You can apply this technique to deadly phrases, as well as gestures. Make a list of all the things you hate to hear. Ask someone whom you have complete confidence in to read them to you. Observe how a word or phrase, once it reaches your brain, sets off a series of involuntary negative emotional reactions in you. Make the person repeat the word or phrase as many time as is necessary for you to be able to hear it calmly, without any negative reaction. When this occurs, you will be free of this particular source of automatic suffering.

We can deal with all the switches that set off negative reactions in this way. However, this technique for desensitising yourself is more appropriate to a group therapy or seminar situation, and is not as easily applied at home, on your own. That's why I am proposing a second approach, which can easily be done in your own home.

How to re-programme yourself

Another way to deal with the problem of negative automatic reactions is to make the same switch set off a different, and more positive response. In other words, you can re-programme yourself, replacing one automatic response with another. Here's how to proceed:

A. Make a list of situations which you know provoke a negative reaction in you, and which cause you to harm yourself, your environment and the people around you. Do you get angry when your child starts playing with his / her food? Do you get upset when you're driving, and someone doesn't let you pass? Include everything that makes you angry, or afraid, or that you want to hide about yourself...

B. When the list is finished (you can always add to it later) look at each provocation, and ask yourself what disadvantages your reactions have for you? Can you continue reacting automatically, or would it be more advantageous for you to change or get rid of this programme?

C. Now that you know what needs to be done, you should ask yourself what kind of reaction you'd like as a substitute. For example, when my child plays with his food, I'd like to be able to stay calm, and say something in an encouraging tone of voice, something like, "Don't you think it would be just as much fun to use your fork?" Write each of these alternatives down.

D. This done, visualise each situation in your mind, and repeat your positive response, in the present tense, as many times as you need to make it automatic.

You will find a useful compliment to this technique in the section on self affirmation, a little later on.

Mental and emotional shields

We become what we think

Concentrate on pain, and you become that pain. Concentrate on light, and you become luminous. Repeat to yourself, "This is impossible..." and whatever it is will remain impossible. Say to yourself, "I can do it..." and your chances of success will increase a hundredfold.

Say, for example, that you're out for a walk and come across a gully. The only way over is to jump. The gully is about a yard wide. You'd jump it with ease if the distance were only two lines marked on the pavement. But here you're faced with a dangerous, possibly fatal drop if you fail. If you start thinking, "I'm going to fall... I'm going to fall..." then you'd certainly be better off turning around and going home. But if you think, "This is easy..." then you won't have anything to worry about. Before you know it, you'll be on the other side.

I can already hear the objections of skeptics who will say, "Oh, this is just another one of those positive thinking ideas... As if all

I have to do to become a millionaire is to think like a millionaire!" If you're one of these people, then it's probably because somewhere inside you, you have a firm belief that, "It won't work... it won't work..." and so, of course, it won't work for you!

Self fulfilling prophecy

A researcher by the name of Dr. Coue discovered a psychological phenomenon which was subsequently studied by other psychologists, and which they described as the "cycle of self reinforcement." We tend to influence events in a way that is in accordance with our beliefs. For example, take an elderly person who believes s/he is incapable of using a video cassette recorder. The person believes that... "It's too complicated for me..." or "I was never any good with electric gadgets..." or "I can't start learning about these things at my age..."

Say the person gets a video recorder as a gift. You can imagine what happens. Despite all the instructions and help offered by the salesperson, children, friends, etc. and despite a clearly written manual on how to use the machine, the elderly person in question just can't seem to grasp the principles of how to use it on his / her own, and says, "You see, I told you so!"

People have this amazing capacity to fulfil their own prophecies. Especially when the prophecies are positive. In such cases, the person's forces are buoyed by hope. As you may suppose, there's nothing magic about all this. Human beliefs cannot defy natural laws (except for miracles). It isn't enough to say, "I am healthy..." to cure cancer, but thinking it can help considerably. There haven't been any cases recorded so far of someone throwing themselves out of a twentieth story window, and floating gently down to the ground, simply because they repeated, "I am as light as a feather..."

However, if we take a closer look at the issue, we must admit that if people today are able to fly for hours on air currents, supported by a bit of nylon and a few lengths of aluminium tubing, without the help of a motor (delta-planing), it's because long long ago, a fool named Icarus believed he could fly...

If you want more - say it!

As we've just seen, you carry around all kinds of affirmations about all kinds of subjects. Some of these affirmations can be called "beliefs" while others are "prejudices," or "opinions" or "judgments." Whatever they are, you conceived most of them unconsciously, without concerning yourself about their effects on your behaviour, and in a general sense, on your life and on the lives of the people around you.

Some of these affirmations have a harmful effect on your health, or on your capacity to communicate with others and get what you want out of life. Others have a beneficial effect.

It is very useful to know that you can create conscious affirmations, which help you maintain a positive attitude towards the goals and objectives you set for yourself in life. To do this you just have to follow a few rules, which will guarantee their effectiveness, making them powerful and efficient tools.

How to create effective affirmations

The rules to follow have been described so many times that we can almost assume most people know them already. Nevertheless, we will repeat them here. Let's use the example of an affirmation that is an excellent emotional shield: No matter what anyone says or does to me, I am a worthy human being...

A. Personal: Using the first person "I" assures that you identify yourself with the affirmation. Saying "I am a worthy person..." establishes this is a true fact for you, which would not be the case if you said something like, "You have to have courage in order to..."

B. Present tense: Even if the affirmation refers to a future event, it should be formulated in the present tense. For example, if you want to remain calm next time you encounter a difficult person, do not formulate your affirmation as, "I will stay calm the next time..." because when the situation does arise, you will once again think, "Next time, I'll stay calm..." (but not this time!). This is a little like the famous sign posted by a shopkeeper: No credit today - only tomorrow.

Affirmations influence our subconscious mind, where only the present exists. In order for them to be effective when and where you need them, they must be conceived and engraved in your mind as if they were valid from the present moment on. For example, "I am calm..." or "I face the situation courageously..."

C. Positive: Another characteristic of your subconscious is that it has trouble differentiating between a thing, and the negation of that thing. For example, if I mention the word "dog" the animal comes immediately to mind. But if I ask you not to think about dogs, then what's the first thing that pops into your mind? A dog!

Therefore, if your goal is not to be afraid the next time you encounter an aggressive person, do not formulate your affirmation by saying, "I am not afraid..." because this instils the idea of fear in your mind. Instead, say something like, "I am courageous..."

The rule here is to concentrate on what you want to attain, and not on what you wish to avoid.

D. Categorical: Your affirmations should leave no room for doubt. So avoid comparative or conditional statements. For example, if you say, "Whatever happens, I will be the calmest person around..." then happens if someone else is calmer than you are? Or if you say, "I am calm if necessary..." how can you expect to establish an automatic reaction of staying calm, and a process for evaluating whether staying calm is necessary or not, all at the same time? Your subconscious won't be able to handle it.

So instead, say something like, "I remain calm, whatever happens."

E. Indicate the state you want to attain, and not a gradual progression towards that state. If you say, "I am self confident..." you evoke a feeling that you can easily relate to, by recalling events in your past where you felt confident. However, if you say, "Little by little I gain more self confidence..." then your affirmation loses its power, because your subconscious cannot measure the qualification "little by little." What's more, just because you make progress towards attaining a goal does not necessarily mean you will attain that goal. So in reality, you are not offering yourself any real support, but simply a promise of support some time in the future.

F. Charged with positive emotion: Your affirmation will be stronger if it is charged with positive emotion. Saying, "I have self confidence..." is fine. It occupies your mind with a positive thought, true enough. But saying, "I am self confident, and I love being with people..." is a lot better, because it is charged with emotion. Can you see the difference?

G. Other recommendations: Affirmations are linked to objectives. For example, say you want to acquire more self confidence, stay calm in the face of aggression, and preserve your self esteem despite the attacks you may be subjected to. All these psychological objectives are quite realistic, and there is nothing that can prevent you from attaining them.

Four words to avoid

Be careful about being too much of a perfectionist when you formulate your objectives. Saying "I am always calm and benevolent..." is not realistic - even a Saint couldn't live up to that! You're setting yourself up for not being able to live up to your expectations, and this will only serve to tarnish the credibility of all your affirmations. You have to be realistic, and project a state that can reasonably be attained. Avoid words like always and never, perfectly, totally, etc.

Also be careful to include only yourself in your affirmations. Saying, "I remain calm and make the other person laugh..." will still only affect you, and no one else. Thinking very hard, "I want him to love me..." will not make him love you! You might even provoke an opposite reaction to the one you want. This would follow the "rule of inverse flow" which states that the more we chase after something, the more it seems to elude us. And inversely, as soon as we stop chasing after it, it starts to pursue us!

How to make your affirmations operational

It takes more than just writing an affirmation down to make it work for you, and develop your inner strength. As we have seen, we are already programmed with all kinds of affirmations, many of which were engraved in our minds a long time ago. These have been confirmed and repeated countless times, through the cycle of self reinforcement described earlier.

To inscribe new, supportive affirmations in our subconscious, we have to repeat them and reinforce many many times. There are a number of techniques for doing this:

- First of all, write your affirmation on a small blackboard or piece of cardboard and hang it somewhere that is very visible. This way, you'll look at the message and register it often. Don't write more than one message at a time - this will only confuse your subconscious, and cancel out any positive effect. Work on your objectives one by one. You can change the message when you realise you're not paying any attention to it anymore.

- Another technique for reprogramming your subconscious is to repeat your affirmation in a low voice, over and over again before you fall asleep, and again as soon as you wake up in the morning.

- If you know how to practice visualisation, than you can use the technique to imagine yourself in the process of living out your affirmation. "See" yourself as the confident person you want to be. See yourself in a situation where you feel joyous in the company of others. Repeat the visualisation as often as possible, until it becomes a familiar part of your thoughts.

- Lastly, if you feel up to it, you can use another technique which provides astonishing results. It consists of repeating the affirmation 1000 times, out loud, without stopping. This takes about an hour to do. The best way to count is to use matches. Make one pile of twenty, and another of fifty. Each time you repeat the affirmation, take one match from the pile of fifty. When you've gone through the entire pile, remove one match from the pile of twenty. Then start again on the fifty pile. When the pile of twenty is depleted, you've repeated the message a thousand times (twenty times fifty equals one thousand!).

Repeating the affirmation in this way has a very strong effect. In addition to engraving the message on your mind, you approach a state of trance, the full effects of which we will discuss a little later on.

Affirmations as emotional shields

Affirmations act all on their own. Once implanted in your brain, they automatically produce the desired effect, as we have already seen. However, you can also use affirmations in a conscious way, whenever you're under some kind of intense pressure, particular to a given situation. For example, if you become the object of an especially corrosive type of verbal aggression (say you've made some kind of serious error, and are reprimanded severely for it) you can protect your self image by repeating the message, "Whatever anyone says or does to me, I am a worthy human being..." This is what we call an emotional shield. You grab on to a positive emotion, which is firmly anchored in your mind, whenever negative emotions (fear, anger, shame etc.) threaten to take over.

We cannot experience two emotions or think two thoughts at the same time

We cannot experience two opposing emotions at the same time, nor can we consciously think two thoughts simultaneously. So you can't be happy and afraid at the same time. Nor can you consciously calculate what 72 times 333 is, while thinking about what you're going to say to your boss about coming in late yesterday morning.

This phenomenon explains how you can protect yourself against negative emotions during your encounters with difficult people. You can neutralise your negative thoughts or feelings, simply by thinking about something else. If you succeed in building a solid defence of positive feelings and thoughts, which are able to resist encroachment by disturbing negative emotions and thoughts, then you will become strong and serene, and master of yourself.

The power of paradox

Say you are having problems with your immediate superior. He calls you into his office, and you know that once again you're in for a lecture about all the supposed mistakes you made, and that you're going to get into an argument as you try to defend yourself. These encounters have always ended badly in the past. Your superior has always been able to throw you off balance, until you lost your temper and stormed out in a huff.

But this time you've decided that you're going to follow the advice offered in this book, and remain impassive, no matter what happens. However, you know that what your superior says is going to hurt you, and you'd love to find a way to avoid being hurt. What can you do?

One possibility is to repeat a sentence like, "Whatever he says or does to me, I am still a worthy human being..." to yourself, before, and during the encounter. This is an effective measure, because with this idea ingrained in your mind, you can remain neutral in the face of criticism and attack by twenty such people. But this is a purely defensive position, and there may be a more effective way to deal with the situation.

You get to the meeting on time, but your superior makes you wait in the hallway for a full thirty minutes, without giving any reason for the delay. You know he's just trying to exert his authority, and set you up for what's to come. Finally, you're admitted to his office. He's on the phone, and pretends he doesn't see you come in, so you have to stand there waiting some more. Finally, he tells you to sit down on a hard, straight backed chair, which places you in a distinctly inferior position, compared to his imposing desk and padded armchair. He grills you with an intimidating look, and then begins his attack, assuming that you are psychologically vulnerable.

Attacking your self esteem

All the manoeuvres described above are aimed at attacking your self esteem. The person probably sees you as a threat, and needs to reduce you to a state of submission. Showing a lack of respect or getting angry would be a mistake on your part, since this is exactly what the person wants you to do. He knows perfectly well how to exploit your anger in order to destroy you.

However, this time you're well aware of the purpose behind his odious strategy. You find the man mean, petty and mediocre, yet you're aware that for some reason you've been placed in a position where he has power over you, and over your career. You're fuming inside, at the thought of the trap he is trying to set for you. Having been treated so badly, you're tempted to come down to his level, and respond in kind. But you know that this would only make him happy - there's nothing he'd like better than for you to lose control, get angry, and leave the meeting defeated and depressed.

An infallible response

There is an infallible way to respond to this kind of antagonism. Formulate a kind of blessing in your mind, something like, "May God bless you..." It doesn't matter if you have absolutely no belief in God. Neither does it matter that you have no desire to bless the person in question. The thought itself has so much power that it works all on its own. Try it! Repeat this sentence in your mind, and at the same time try to evoke hateful thoughts about someone. It's impossible. Remember, you can't think or feel two opposing things at the same time. So you can't bless someone, and hate them simultaneously.

You don't even have to put any feeling into it. If you can maintain the thought, "May God bless him..." firmly in your mind, you'll be floating three feet above his desk, throughout the meeting! He'll make his nasty insinuations, and you'll repeat your blessing. Which of the two is stronger, do you think?

Repeating this (or a similar) formula will change your outlook. You'll cease feeling spiteful or nervous, and although you may be the victim of all kinds of abuse, you'll remain serene and impassive, beyond the reach of petty aggression. And this will serve to upset the other person completely!

The power of incantations

You may have seen images on TV of young soldiers throwing themselves fearlessly into the line of enemy fire, chanting the name of God. They seem to be in a trance, and nothing can stop them. Such is the power of incantation, when it is charged with emotional fervour. The words used in these incantations are often words of praise for some divinity, endlessly repeated, to the point where there is no room for anything else in the person's mind: no room for doubt, or even for an awareness of the person's own identity.

An almost superhuman force

We can easily imagine the almost superhuman force that such practice produces. The problem is that it can be used to make persons do things against their will, in which case it closely resembles the brainwashing techniques used so effectively by totalitarian governments. But the truth is that in most cases, subjects submit willingly to this kind of conditioning. They use it to find a way of escaping from the sad reality of their own lives. This is the danger of any kind of religious fanaticism or fundamentalism, which offers power and release to those who practice repeating incantations, and eventually experience the resulting state of trance.

But this power is not the exclusive property of religion. If you learn to make conscious use of the incantation technique whenever you are faced with verbal or mental aggression, you can protect yourself. The incantation could be an affirmation that you've repeated to yourself a thousand times, and which thus becomes available to you whenever you need it. It could be a series of sounds or syllables, like the "mantras" taught by Oriental spiritual masters. However if you want to use a mantra, it's better to be taught one directly, by a spiritual master.

The power of disassociation

Modern psychology has taken over the role of religious sects in developing techniques to help us increase our inner strength. It proposes that for each difficult situation, there are a number of possible reactions. Either we find ourselves IN the situation, and therefore experience the emotions it provokes, associating ourselves with those emotions. Or we maintain an attitude of observer, thereby disassociating ourselves from the experience.

The more a person gets involved with an experience, the more s/he is associated with it, and the stronger the emotions s/he feels. It could be a situation that is happening in the present, or one that is only a memory, but which left a deep mark on the person when it did take place. The problem we're dealing with in this chapter is precisely that of being too emotionally involved in a situation, i.e. too associated, and therefore incapable of taking any positive, meaningful action. The objective, then, is to learn how to keep your distance.

How to remain disassociated

To illustrate the technique, we will refer once again to the example of the nasty superior described earlier. You're sitting there in his office, in the chair which symbolises your inferior position. How can you remain disassociated in this situation?

The key here is your ability to visualise and use your creative imagination. The most important thing is to be able to play around with your perception of the person facing you. Distance is important - if you're just a couple of feet away, try to move your chair back a little. Now imagine that you're looking at this person through the wrong end of a telescope - he looks very small, minuscule in fact, although you're both in the same room.

Problems overwhelm us when we perceive them as being larger than we are. There's the expression… "making a mountain out of a molehill." Imagining these problems as smaller than we are simply requires imagining that we are larger than they. If the person you're talking to is your immediate problem, then imagine that you are Gulliver, and he is a resident of Lilliput. Your body is immense, his tiny. This simple thought alone will do much to neutralise his power over you.

Switch places

Putting yourself in someone else's shoes means understanding what is going on inside that person's head. It doesn't mean you become the other person, or agree with him.

Switching places means temporarily adopting the other person's point of view, and trying to see, hear and think the way s/he does.

What we may perceive as negative, aberrant, or destructive behaviours in other persons are simply inappropriate ways of satisfying their legitimate needs and desires. What we find disturbing in other people generally results from their efforts to fulfil a deep-seated need, or to live up to an unconscious value system, ingrained in their personalities since childhood.

Realising this enables you to make a distinction between "behaviour" and "intention." By putting yourself in the other person's shoes, you can discover what it is that really needs to be satisfied in your relations with that person. Other people have the same problems that you do: their intentions may overshoot their actions. If you make them aware of it, they will have to come out and say something like, "I was misunderstood, misinterpreted..." or "That wasn't my intention, I'm so sorry..."

To understand someone, you must know what their intentions are, what value system or criteria form the basis of their behaviour, especially when that behaviour is problematical to you. If you can do this, then you are in a position to suggest other alternatives, which fulfil the person's requirements, and which are also acceptable to you.

But it's hard enough becoming aware of your own deep-seated intentions. Wouldn't other people's underlying intentions be even harder to determine? No, because it's easier to observe and understand others than it is to observe and understand yourself! We are often blind to certain aspects of our own personality, which are completely obvious to others.

However, doing this requires an ability to concentrate on someone else and perceive subtle signs, as well as ask the right kinds of questions, at the right time. Mastering these techniques will cause a large portion of your communication problems to disappear.

Visualisation exercise

Our capacity for creative imagination (including visualisation) should be developed. When we are children, our imaginations are much stronger. As we grow older, we replace imagination with improved reasoning, which is necessary if we are to control our emotions.

Here is a sample visualisation exercise to help you "put yourself in someone else's shoes." It will also help you develop your ability to visualise. You can't do the exercise properly by reading the text for yourself. Try to find someone to read it for you (in a calm, clear voice) or tape it yourself, and then play it back during the exercise. You can also order it on cassette, from the publisher of this book.

"Get comfortable in a quiet place. Don't cross your arms or legs. Close your eyes, and concentrate on your eyelids, and especially on the muscles around your eyes. Relax these muscles slowly. Let this feeling of relaxation spread through your body. Breathe in deeply... now breathe out, repeating the number 7 in your mind, and imagining the colour red.

Relax your entire body, from head to foot. Let your body go. You feel a pleasant wave of relaxation spreading through your whole body.

Breathe in deeply... As you breathe out, repeat the number 6 in your mind, and imagine the colour orange. By controlling your thoughts, you control your emotions.

You only want what is good for you.

Breathe in deeply... Then, as you breathe out, repeat the number 5 in your mind, and visualise the colour yellow. Calm your mind. Feel your mind relaxing, resting. Breathe in deeply, and as you exhale, repeat the number 4 to yourself, visualising the colour green. A profound feeling of peace pervades you. Think of the word "serenity." You are serene...

Take another deep breathe, and then as you breathe out, repeat the number 3 to yourself, and visualise the colour blue. A feeling of love pervades your being. You are one with love.

Breathe in again, slowly and deeply, and as you breathe out, repeat the number 2 to yourself, and visualise the colour indigo. You are discovering the real source of your being. You are in harmony with yourself.

Take another deep breathe... As you breathe out slowly, repeat the number 1 in your mind, and visualise the colour violet. You are in touch with the deepest part of your being. the innermost levels of your mind, and you can use this energy to accomplish whatever you desire, as long as your goal is consistent with your values, and is something you sincerely want.

Now use your creative imagination to visualise a large sphere of white light... the sphere is floating above your head, radiating beautiful golden-white light... You are bathed in the warmth of this light... let it fill you completely, let it surround you and protect you... in this state, only things which are for your greatest good can happen to you... you feel all your negativity flowing out of you... replaced by light... let all your negativity go...

Now search your memory for some difficult situation that you experienced, either in your professional or private life.

In this situation, you have a problem with someone.

The relationship is bad. An argument, a disagreement or some other kind of aggression is taking place.

The scene becomes clearer and clearer in your mind.

Specify when it took place... where it happened... the name of the other person...

You observe the scene.

You hear what is said, as well as any other sounds in the area.

You re-experience the feelings you had during, and after the difficult situation...

Maybe you associate some special odour or taste with the situation...

Take your time, and try to recall everything associated with the event in your mind...

Now take a step back and observe the scene. You see it as an independent and objective observer.

You see yourself, standing or sitting, facing the person you're having problems with.

Look at the person more carefully. Keep on seeing, hearing and feeling the person in your mind.

Now enter the mind of that person.

You're inside the mind of the person you're having a problem with. You see yourself through this person's eyes, hear yourself through his / her ears, feel what s/he feels. You see yourself facing the person, through the lenses of his / her eyes.

Now you enter the thoughts of the person, asking yourself, "What is my positive intention in opposing (say your name...)?

- What don't I like about (say you r name)?
- What disturbs me? What irritates me about (your name)?
- What is at stake for me?
- What do I stand to gain?
- What do I stand to lose?
- What am I really trying to achieve by behaving this way?

Answer these questions in your mind, without forcing anything.

Pay attention to all your thoughts, even the most unusual or obscure ones, for they often carry the seeds of truth.

Continue to think as if you were the other person, and ask yourself this question: "Isn't there any other way I can reach my objective, or satisfy my need in this situation?" Try to come up with an alternative solution.

You're still inside the person you're having a problem with. You see through his / her eyes, and perhaps you see your own face, as if you were looking at yourself in a mirror, through the lenses of the other person's eyes.

You are thinking for the other person, and you ask yourself, "What else could I do to fulfil my needs?"

And you try to find a second solution - a second option.

You're still thinking as if you were the person you're having trouble with. S/he now has two other possible solutions, aside from arguing with you or trying to dominate you. Formulate these options clearly in your mind.

- Now how do you feel in the other person's position?
- Do you see your adversary (you) in the same way?
- Now it's time to leave the other person's body.
- You are an external observer once again. You still see the two people, yourself and the other, facing each other.
- Do you notice any change in the relationship? It's now time to close the file and separate yourself from the persons involved in this little scene.

In a moment, I'm going to ask you to open your eyes. When you do open your eyes, you will be completely awake, and feel in perfect health.

Your head and neck will be relaxed.

You'll feel in harmony with life.

When you feel ready, become fully aware of where you are... of your presence here in this room... you feel the surface you're sitting or lying on... wiggle your toes, contract and relax the muscles in your legs. Move your jaw around... Clench your fists slowly, then release them. Breathe in deeply. Stretch your whole body. When you're ready, open your eyes... you are completely awake, and in perfect health..."

Now, before you say anything, take a pen and paper and write down all the information you learned during this visualisation exercise.

Physical techniques for controlling emotion

Scientific research has shown that each emotion is characterised by a specific respiratory rhythm. Therefore, emotions modify the way you breathe, and if you voluntarily control your breathing, you can modify, or control, your emotions. The two are closely linked.

On a practical level, it has long been known that practising deep breathing (filling the stomach and chest cavities) has a powerful soothing effect. This kind of breathing is accomplished by relaxing the abdominal muscles (solar plexus) and filling first the stomach, then the chest with air, instead if just the chest. This is how we breathe when we're calm or resting, and doing it consciously results in our becoming calm and rested.

Another way of reducing tension in difficult situations consists of focussing a part of your attention on pleasant physical sensations: smoking a cigarette, being aware of the feel of a chair or table to the touch, feeling the contact of your feet planted firmly on the ground, and so on.

Finally, we know that emotions are linked to hormonal reactions and secretions, which produce all kinds of physical effects, a phenomenon we understand all too well when we suffer an attack of stagefright. An excellent way to control these effects is to practise dynamic relaxation.

Dynamic Relaxation

As its name indicates, the principle behind dynamic relaxation is to get relaxed through movement. The idea is to mobilise your body to get rid of the excess accumulation of hormones, and especially of adrenalin. You can do this by shaking your head like a dog coming out of water, or yawning and working your jaw around, or by pacing around until you calm down. You can also do a simple massage on yourself, which works like this:

Roll your head around from right to left, in a circular movement, and stretch your neck. Doing this will make you feel like massaging the nape of your neck with your hands... do so.

Stretching your neck also stretches your shoulder muscles, and you feel like massaging them too. You can do this by crossing your hands to the opposite shoulders, and using your thumb and index fingers. These muscles are usually painfully sensitive, because of the toxins that accumulate there. Knead the muscles on both sides, strongly enough to cause some pain. Then massage them with the tips of your fingers.

This massage should make you shiver right down your spine. Lift your shoulders, then relax and let them fall again. Breathe in deeply, then breathe out in a long sigh.

Doing these simple exercises before a difficult encounter should relax you sufficiently to put you in a positive frame of mind, so that you can deal with the situation more effectively, and remain in control of your emotions.

You have all the resources you need

The more progress science makes in understanding human beings, the more apparent it becomes that each person possesses the necessary resources to overcome any problem, and take control of his / her life. We don't need someone to solve our problems for us.

Instead we need people who can show us how to locate, in ourselves, the resources necessary to solve the problem at hand. Think of the old Chinese proverb that says: "Give a hungry person a fish, and he'll eat once; teach him how to fish, and he'll eat for the rest of his life."

Many of our fears and limitations were actually formed during childhood. For example, you may have been impressed by an authoritarian adult, and felt yourself tiny in comparison. But you continue to be influenced by authority, even though you're all grown up, as if the part of you that is afraid is forever linked to that event in the past. To free yourself of this fear, all you have to do is talk to the child you were, the child who is still inside you, and inform him / her that you are now a fully grown adult, and that s/he no longer need be afraid.

Where do we hide our courage?

On the other hand, we sometimes exhibit marvellous qualities which seem to be sorely lacking under other circumstances. How is it possible to have the courage to face the wind and the waves on a windsurfer, for example, yet find ourselves sweating it out for hours before we get up enough guts to confront a difficult situation, say before calling someone we know will be argumentative? Where do we hide our courage during these kinds of difficult situations?

Experiments in contemporary physiology have shown that individuals require only one single repetition of an event for a reaction to become permanent. For example, once you learn to ride a bicycle, you'll always know how to do it, even if you don't touch one for fifty years. In the same way, if you have been an enthusiastic person, courageous, dynamic, balanced, serene etc. in just one situation in your life, that is enough for you to continue to know and retain that quality throughout your life, even if you don't use it again.

This technique will help you call upon those inner resources when you need them:

Visualisation : Accessing a resource

Get comfortable in a quiet place... don't cross your arm or legs. Close your eyes and breathe in deeply; as you breathe out, let all the tension flow out of your body. Take another deep breathe, and as you breathe out, get rid of all your mental tension. Now breathe normally, and let the feeling of total relaxation pervade your body and your mind...

Now think of a difficult situation that you are worried about, because you don't feel you have what it takes to deal with it effectively.

Which quality - which inner resource - would you like to have in this situation?

Now look for a situation in the past where you exhibited that inner resource. It doesn't matter what kind of situation, as long as you experienced the quality you are seeking. Relive the experience in your mind, in as much detail as possible.

Was it in a place full of light? Or was it in some dark room? If it was dark, turn the lights up higher.

Now try to become aware of the quality or resource you showed at that time. Slowly close one of your hands. The more you feel that quality or resource, the tighter you clench your fist.

Now open your fist slowly. Keep your eyes shut.

Now try to remember another situation where you exhibited the same quality. Visualise the scene... If you can't find one, go back to the first and do it over again.

Concentrate on how you felt as you demonstrated the quality, the resource you are seeking. Slowly close the same hand as before. The more you feel the quality you seek, the tighter you clench your fist.

Now open your fist slowly, and let your mind relax for a moment.

Close your fist again, and reinforce the positive experience you've just had.

Note: After this exercise, the simple act of closing your fist should put you in touch with the quality or resource you were seeking: courage, patience, serenity, enthusiasm, or any other quality you choose. If this doesn't happen, you'll have to repeat the visualisation, trying to find a past experience where you felt the quality very strongly, and then concentrating on it as intensely as possible, while slowly clenching your fist.

Make a mental projection of yourself, in a situation in the near future where you will need this quality. Try to imagine how the difficult situation will take place. Imagine yourself in the situation, and then slowly clench your fist. Concentrate on the quality that the gesture is linked to... the quality you need now...

Now come back to yourself; become aware of the surface on which you are sitting or lying; wriggle your toes, contract and relax your leg muscles; move your jaw around; clench your fists slowly. Breathe in deeply. Stretch your body. When you're ready, open your eyes... You are fully awake, and you feel in perfect health...

Close your fist as before: you feel the the quality you were seeking inside you. It was there in the past, and it's there now, ready to be used...

Note: The more situations a quality is linked to, the stronger it becomes. So it would be a good idea to repeat this visualisation as many times as necessary to gain a firm grip on the quality you are seeking. Remember to use the same hand for only one quality at a time.

This technique for linking and accessing inner resources is based on the unconscious association of an external physical stimulus and an internal state of mind. You can use other external stimuli, besides the clenched fist: pressing your thumb on any part of your body - always making sure it's the same stimulus for the same quality - or any other tactile stimulus. The link could also be triggered by an image or a sound, but they are harder to set up when doing the visualisation exercise on your own, with your eyes closed.

CHAPTER 9
The Supreme Weapon: Humour!

"A thief broke into a house and started carting away almost everything he could find. The legitimate owner, who was in the street talking to some friends, saw the man come and go, loaded with his belongings. He waited a few minutes, then went into his house, covered himself with a blanket and pretended he was sleeping.

"What are you doing there," asked the thief when he came back for another load.

"Well," said the man, "we're moving, aren't we?" (Story told by Nasrudin, Idries Shah)

We all know how a burst of shared laughter can brighten up the most sombre of days. We've experienced the magic of laughter from childhood on, when our little smiles and acrobatics seemed to cause such joy in those around us.

We continued having a lot of fun during adolescence, when almost anything could provoke a round of giggling. We were sometimes accused of being "childish" by adults who couldn't understand our euphoria. Not to mention those bouts of uncontrolled hilarity that swept us away from time time, and which no one or anything could stop.

However, it wasn't until later in life that we really learned how to make use of humour, i.e. to look at situations and events with amused detachment.

The essence of humour

Seeing the humour in situations or events makes you realise that, in a sense, life is a joke. But more than that, it helps you take the drama out of situations, and understand that they're only as important as you make them out to be.

Say you lose something you consider valuable. If you consider the loss serious, then it becomes a tragedy. If you can laugh about it, then you understand that it is within your power to see the situation is a comedy, a game, a farce. The essence of humour lies in the unreal nature of things. To grasp this concept, just think about things that have made you laugh in the past. Take those TV programmes that use a hidden camera. What we find funny is people's astonished reactions to unexpected or impossible situations.

A young man goes to open the door of his car, which he left in a parking lot a short time before. The door handle comes off in his hand. He's so surprised that he remains speechless for a moment. For us, the spectators, his reaction is the funniest thing imaginable, because we know that the scene has been staged.

But why is this scene funny? It's funny because we are witnessing a spectacle in which someone mistakes an illusion for reality. The same thing happens when we see a man in the street reacting to a beautiful woman, running towards him with open arms. We see his responses: his face brightens with expectation, then sags as the woman runs past him into the arms of another man, who appears in the background.

This isn't at all funny to the man who was tricked. But it is for us, because we know that the scene is an illusion, a setup.

What if everything were illusion?

A case in point

I'll always remember a young woman who told her story during a seminar I'd attended. She'd been severely victimised, and the story could only be perceived as tragic.

As a young newlywed, she gave birth to a child, whom she loved dearly. However, her husband soon began to show signs of manic jealousy, to the point where he kept her locked up in the house for an entire year. She finally managed to escape with her child, and went to her parents for refuge. Her husband followed her, and threatened her with all kinds of harm, including death, until one day he cut open his wrists in her presence, and smeared his blood all over the walls of her parents' house. A short time later, he kidnapped the child and fled to the country where he was born. He swore to the woman that she'd never see her child again.

A year had passed since the events which left the young woman completely resigned and depressed. She was desperately sad at being separated from her child, and she had nightmares about her husband's attempted suicide.

When she had to tell her story during the seminar, stripped of any elements except those she'd provoked herself, we thought it would be impossible for her to do so, the situation being so dramatic.

However, the exercise forced her to look at the situation from a different perspective, something she hadn't ever tried to do before. And suddenly she burst out laughing. She imagined her husband as a tragically comic clown, instead of a menacing ogre. She pitied him. She retold the scene of her husband's suicide as if it were some pompous theatrical farce... why her husband didn't even have to go to the hospital afterwards! Her laughter was infectious, and soon the whole room was in an uproar.

A short time later, she went and took back her child herself, and in the face of her determination, her husband didn't dare do anything to stop her.

Humour can smash obsessions

Well then, tragedy or comedy? Who decides? Not the facts themselves, that's certain. Facts need to be interpreted to make any sense.

The events this woman lived through were becoming an obsession for her. That means she kept seeing the same events over and over again in her mind, running the same film endlessly, without being able to find a solution to her problem. The obsession could have become permanent, and very serious. Laughter smashed her obsession instantaneously. And, like Sleeping Beauty, she awoke from her nightmare, free of her suffering.

Humour challenges conditioned ideas

As we've just seen, humour can sometimes take the drama out of tragic or macabre situations. We talk about "black" humour. But whether black or white, humour always challenges accepted ideas, and plays with the essential difference, or gap, between reality and the way it is expressed.

Some people totally lack a sense of humour. This can be due to retarded intelligence, or to a conscious effort to take everything seriously, which amounts to the same thing.

You may think that taking things seriously makes you more important, or gives you more credibility. To reassure yourself, go to a zoo and watch the monkeys for awhile: they usually look as serious as a president at a press conference. But monkeys only look serious because they itch all the time, and are trying not to scratch! Having a sense of humour means being able to get outside of yourself and look at yourself objectively, and therefore NOT take yourself too seriously, i.e. being able to laugh at yourself.

This also allows you to deal with serious issues, while not identifying yourself with them - you maintain a certain distance, or gap, between the issues and yourself. This makes them much easier to deal with, for everyone involved.

Even bitter humour is a liberating force

Humour usually provokes a smile rather than outright laughter. We rarely experience pure joyous laughter, because laughing is often partly cruel, as we are forced to give up some illusion we've been holding on to. As you know, it's sometimes difficult to abandon beliefs which we've held for a long time, and which have become extremely important to us.

However, humour is an immensely powerful liberating force. The moment a painful illusion, which has been making us suffer, dissolves in a burst of humour, the burden associated with it in our minds also disappears.

When can we make use of humour?

Your sense of humour will be an important resource in your dealings with difficult people. You will use it to take the drama out of situations and neutralise other people's aggressiveness.

Let's look at a few examples of delicate situations, where humour can come in handy:

- 1. When you want to say "No" without offending someone.

- 2. When you're obsessed by a problem, and can only think of the usual solutions. Humour can help you reformulate the problem, and break out of your unproductive cycle of thinking.

- 3. When working very hard as part of a team, trying to meet a deadline, tensions can mount and make people irritable and mean. Have you ever noticed that people who spend long hours working against the clock often need to sit around and tell stupid jokes about anything and everything afterwards? This is simply a way of releasing tension - humour acts as a safety valve.

- 4. During a conflict, when negotiations have reached an impasse, humour can clear away obstacles and incite people to move from their entrenched positions and clean the slate. It opens new lines of communication.

- 5. You want to reach people who have turned a deaf ear so far. Humour can attract attention, without hurting anyone.

- 6. When we want to make someone feel comfortable. Cordial good humour can overcome barriers of age, education, social standing, diverse interests, etc.

- 7. When you have to speak in public, humour helps you relax and capture people's attention.

We can see from these examples that humour is a precious element for successful interpersonal relations.

How to sharpen your sense of humour

A sense of humour is directly linked to the ability to play, and is indispensable for any kind of creative thought. To sharpen your sense of humour, you must, first of all, allow yourself to play.

For example, do you consider work some kind of divine punishment, or do you think that the ideal kind of work is the kind that's fun to do?

Do you think problems exist in order to ruin your existence, or to stimulate your imagination?

How much importance do you place on creativity and game playing in your life?

Give your laughing muscles a workout

If you're the type of person who has a hearty laugh at least once a day, then you don't need to read this section.

But few people are sufficiently happy or fulfilled, or oblivious enough of their problems, to laugh even as often as once a day.

Most people don't have that many occasions to rejoice. This section concerns them.

One thing is certain: humour makes people laugh, or at least smile, the difference being simply a question of degree. You can laugh alone: you've surely found yourself laughing out loud when reading, hearing or seeing something funny. You can make others laugh too. But to amuse others, you first have to amuse yourself. Laughing is contagious, in the same way that boredom or sadness is contagious. It's impossible for you to use your sense of humour if you don't laugh regularly on your own.

Laughing requires the contraction of two main sets of facial muscles: the major zygomatic muscles, which pull the corners of the mouth upwards, and the buccinal muscles which pull the lower lip upwards, and stretch the mouth.

If you rarely laugh, these muscles undergo a process of atrophy, and you end up with a permanent scowl, even when you laugh. Therefore, you absolutely must do some exercises which make use of all your facial muscles. You can find them described in detail in women's beauty magazines, since in addition to making your face more pleasant and alluring, these exercises help avoid signs of premature aging from appearing on your face.

So every morning before you go out, do some facial exercises, using your muscles to make all kinds of grimaces. This will put a smile on your face and help you stay young. But you can do better than this: go out and take advantage of every occasion you can for laughing.

Avoid bad news

The world seems to be on the brink of disaster, and things appear to be quite desperate, if you centre your attention exclusively on bad news. Famine, war, epidemics, assassinations, natural disasters, fires, racial tensions, torture, injustice... there's not much there to cheer you up!

Mass media inundates us with this kind of information, taking care to mention everything from a train wreck in Asia minor to a flood in Patagonia. The tragic story of the underdog is repeated countless times, and opening a newspaper has become a sure way to get your daily dose of poisonous negativity.

If we add to this the influence of all the complainers and other difficult types whom we've talked about in this book, it's amazing that laughter exists at all any more! What you concentrate on dictates where you end up. If you worry too much about the world's problems, what will be uppermost in your mind? The world's problems! And unfortunately, worrying doesn't contribute much to solving anything. On the contrary...

A wise precaution to take if you want to maintain your capacity to laugh consists of not paying too much to newspaper articles and television reports about various catastrophes, exaggerated by the journalists who write them so that they sell. Some newspapers and magazines even specialise in sensationalising horror: these are to be completely avoided.

As for the rest, is it really necessary to allot so much time to news gathering? If you read a newspaper every day, why not read it twice, or three times a week instead? You will discover that while being no less informed, the dose of toxic negativity you absorb is greatly diminished.

Create an opportunity to laugh every day

Finding occasions to laugh or smile when things are crashing down around you, is not a sign of cynicism or indifference. On the contrary, it keeps the flame burning, revives the spirit in the shadow of adversity, and thus provides human beings with a service which is hard to equal.

You can share in the benefits of laughter, lighten up the environment and the people around you with your contagious joy. Decide to do so from now on. Welcome to the club! Distance yourself from morose people, and try to stay in touch with people who like to laugh, even when problems arise.

Go to funny movies. Read funny books, get tapes of comedians, and so on. Watch your favourite funny programmes on TV. The more you laugh, the easier it gets to laugh more! If you concentrate on the funny things in life, what do you think will preoccupy your mind? Laughter! Forget about doomsday, and enjoy the rest of your life!

In addition, to sharpen your sense of humour, you can apply a few classical methods of creativity in solving your problems.

Exercise: Cutting through the drama

A. Start by recalling a difficult situation, either present or past. Describe the situation in writing, in a few lines. For example:

"When I returned from overseas after an absence of some years, I started looking around for a job. I was called in to a lot of interviews, after which I'd always get a letter saying something like, "We're sorry to inform you that after further consideration, you have not been chosen as for the position. We will keep your application on file, in case any other positions become available in future." After awhile, I really felt like I was walking around with a cross on my shoulders..."

Taken at face value, this is a serious (and rather dull) story. How can it be made humorous?

B. Consider the same problem from various points of view that cut through the drama, that break the problem wide open and allow you to gain some initial distance.

- Exaggerating: here you exaggerate, extend and dramatise the facts to an extreme. You present them in a disproportionate, monstrous light.

"When I returned from overseas, I found I'd been gone so long I didn't even know what kind of money was being used here!" Etc.

- Diminish the facts: here you miniaturise, reduce, shrink, subtract and diminish the original facts concerning the situation in question:

"I started looking for a job, any kind of little job at all. Really, I had no pretensions about finding anything interesting. Just some insignificant position, that would pay me ten thousand dollars a month, and provide eight weeks paid vacation a year…"

- Reverse the roles: In this operation, you imagine that the roles are reversed, that you are the one who is refusing to accept the jobs. You contradict yourself, and oppose everything that seems obvious. In other words, you exaggerate in an inverse sense.

"I was called in by so many people who were fascinated with my person. They were insatiably curious, and I tried to satisfy them, at least at first. Soon I started interrogating the interviewers. I made them understand that it was up to them to convince me that I should accept the job. There was even one who broke down and started crying after two and a half hours of talking, confessing that he couldn't stand his own job any longer…"

- Suppress an element of the problem: this serves to place each element of the problem under scrutiny and, ultimately, to eliminate it completely, giving the situation an absurd or burlesque character.

"After awhile, I realised that I didn't have to work at all, since I was getting along pretty well on the income I received from various sources, which providence had deemed fit to provide me with. But the insane machine was already in motion, and I kept getting these calls to appear at job interviews. Even though I had no interest in acquiring the job, I went anyway because I didn't want to be an added source of frustration for the interviewers…"

- Find unexpected links: we're used to establishing a link between a glass and the act of drinking, for example. Or between a door and an entrance to a building. Change these habitual links, and we come up with items like "a musical glass" or "a door to eternity."

"I would always end up getting a letter which said, "You are so skilled that we don't have a job important enough for you." I got so many of these letters, that I didn't have to buy any toilet paper for some months…"

Now it's your turn…

How can humour help you say "No"?

1. You gain time

Getting the other person to smile or chuckle gives you time to organise your thoughts and prepare your arguments. It helps neutralise tension and anxiety, both your own and the other person's.

2. Humour prevents a loss of face

Your superior asks you to stay and work late. You'd prefer to refuse, but you don't want to antagonise him, especially since there are a number of people present. You know that he is very quick to lose his temper. So your refusal would have to be very, very diplomatic.

How could you respond?

"I'd really like to stay late, sir, but you know after seven o'clock I have a tendency to start adding zero's to numbers! If we want to safeguard the interests of the company, it might be better if I waited until Saturday morning to finish the job. What do you think?" No one has lost face. Everyone in the office has a good laugh, and your superior gets the message, without having any reason to get upset.

3. Humour eases tension

Someone wants something from you which you're not willing to give. It could be your time or participation. You can use humour to ease tension, and at the same time make the other person understand that your refusal is not a question of bad intentions. This is especially important if you had to refuse the same person before, under similar circumstances.

An example:

You're expecting ten persons for dinner, and you've set aside the entire day for getting things ready. Someone calls in the morning and asks for a few hours of your time. It may be your boss, wanting you to look over some files; it may be a client who needs some urgent work; it may be your mother, who wants you to take her shopping.

Whatever your relationship with the person, you can use a variation of the following technique:

"I know you need me today," you say calmly, "and if you can call a caterer and order me dinner for ten, and have it sent over here by 7 o'clock, I'd be happy to help you out." What you're doing is simply answering a request with another (highly unlikely) request, which you make a condition for accepting. You have eased the tension that an outright refusal would have created, and you also avoid causing the other person to lose face.

And if s/he takes you at your word, and decides to cater your party, all the better for you!

4. Humour neutralises aggressiveness

This is perhaps the most important effect of humour. You know how dangerous uncontrolled aggressiveness can be. It can quickly escalate into verbal violence, prevent you from attaining your objectives, and sometimes lead to the loss of friendship, affection and respect of another person.

Humour can help you avoid all that. As soon as you try to be funny, your body relaxes, your expression softens, your face lights up with the flicker of a smile, which makes it very difficult for the other person to maintain a hostile attitude.

Let's look at an example:

You're standing in line at the supermarket, waiting to pay for your week's groceries. The express cash is closed, so you're nice enough to let two people in ahead of you, since they only have one item each. As you're placing your groceries on the counter, a third person comes up and says:

"Would you mind letting me in front? I only have a few things..."

Your first reaction is aggressive. You'd like to say something like: "Yes, I would mind! Get in line like everybody else! I've let enough people in already!"

But fortunately, you call on your sense of humour for help. You keep placing your groceries on the counter and reply, smiling: "My dear lady, I was helping a woman deliver quintuplets this afternoon, when I realised I hadn't gotten anything for dinner tonight. I'd really like to let you in ahead of me, but the fifth baby could pop out at any moment, and I really should get back!"

Or something like this:

"My dear sir, I left my dog watching over a roast beef in the oven at home. If I'm late, he'll eat it, rather than let it go to waste."

The other person will probably start laughing, despite the fact that you're refusing the request, and the problem is solved without any need for hostility.

Resist the temptation to be sarcastic!

Be attentive to your tone of voice. The same joke can be interpreted as a pleasant attempt at humour, or as derision and mockery, depending on the way it is delivered.

Don't make fun of other people

Never make fun of other people. Irony and sarcasm are double-edged swords, because they involve you in a win-lose situation, the dangers of which we've already discussed. You risk setting off an escalation of verbal violence, as the other person understands what you're doing and responds in kind.

On the other hand, cheerful, well-intentioned humour can open many a door that you thought was locked, and get a lot of people on your side.

Now, to give you a more precise idea of how humour can be used to resolve problematical situations, let's look at a few more examples:

A professor is called to the telephone during a class. The students take advantage of his / her absence to climb all over the tables, cover the blackboard with graffiti, vociferate their unruly opinions, etc. The professor returns sooner than expected, finds the class in complete disarray. The class waits apprehensively for the teacher to respond. There is a heavy silence in the air.

"I haven't heard anything like this since the American revolution!" the teacher exclaims. S/he then looks the culprits right in the eye. "You know a lot of people were shot at that time."

Another teacher may have reprimanded the students severely, and sent the worst offenders off to the principal's office, thus creating an atmosphere of tension and fear. But here, the teacher uses laughter to ease tension, restore calm, and get on with the job of educating the students.

Humour in the lion's den

Even the most charismatic persons sometimes have to face a hostile and derisive audience. Say you have some bad news to announce - humour is the only way to get the message across, while keeping your listeners attentive and on your side.

Say a speaker is facing and audience which doesn't seem to be particularly receptive. He already knows that the information he's supposed to deliver is not good news. He clears his throat, and begins:

"When I found out I'd be speaking to you here this afternoon, I thought that if I had the wisdom of Solomon, and the patience of Job, I could maybe avoid the fate of Jonah!"

By making the audience laugh, the orator has already won half the battle.

To conclude this chapter, here's a little story that shows how humour can be used as a way to instruct others about more serious matters: One day, a young student asked a teacher:

"Who did best: the man who conquered an empire, the man who could have conquered an empire but didn't, or the man who prevented someone from conquering an empire?"

"I don't know," the teacher replied, "but what I do know is that there's something more difficult than any of those."

"What?"

"Trying to learn how to see things as they really are." (Nasrudin, Idries Shah)

Conclusion

Well, here we are, at the end of the book. Perhaps you read it right through, from beginning to end. If so, I suggest you go back and read it again, section by section. You'll notice a few things you may have overlooked, things you skipped over, without really registering them consciously.

By following the advice offered here, you will experience a gradual lightening and easing of your day to day tensions. How To Deal With Difficult People is a practical work, which can help you in unexpected ways: you'll gain more self confidence, other people will understand you better, they'll want to help you instead of hinder you, you'll make more friends, etc.

Finally, dealing with difficult people also means dealing with your own fears - dispelling those old demons, and making your life a harmonious experience that others can share in and admire.

This book was structured along the same lines as the seminars I give: it is therefore essentially a practical work. Don't hesitate to make notes, and to add your own experiences to the examples and commentaries. I instructed the publisher to leave wide margins precisely for that reason.

A final word: feel free to write to me and tell me about the results you've obtained by applying these methods. I also welcome any suggestions or criticism. Address your comments to me, care of the publisher, or to the address you'll find at the back of the book. You can be sure that your letter will reach me eventually.

I can only hope that my work will serve to change your life in some positive way - just like mine was turned around - as you apply the techniques for dealing quietly and effectively with difficult people. Now it's up to you. Only you can transform these words into action. Good luck!

Alan Houel

APPENDICES

Appendix To Chapter 2 Passive Aggressiveness

How to deal with people who always say "Yes" but never keep their word

There's another, special kind of aggressive person, whom you may have encountered before: we call this type "passive - aggressive."

These people appear to be generous because they don't know how to say "No." But then, because it's frustrating to always say "yes" when you'd really rather say "no," they build up a lot of resentment against people who ask them for anything.

This kind of aggression, which is often unconscious, is masked by an edict that goes back to childhood, and which says, "Be polite!" It manifests itself in subtle ways: forgotten appointments, work that is overlooked, lateness, unkept promises, etc.

How to make the person keep his / her word

When dealing with a passive-aggressive person, you can't just ask for something and take yes as an answer. You have to go further than that.

- 1. Tell the person why what you're asking is important to you.
- 2. Clarify your request by saying, "Do I have your absolute word that you'll do this by.... (a certain date)?"
- 3. Make the person understand what will happen if s/he doesn't keep his word (in that case, you'll be obliged to...)

- 4. Continue the discussion after an agreement has been reached, and ask the person to repeat what s/he has to do.

- 5. Get it down in writing. Just a simple note of 3 lines is sufficient.

- 6. Don't wait for the deadline to pass before renewing your inquiries. Make sure the person is taking the necessary intermediary steps to fulfil his / her obligation ("How's it going? What have you accomplished so far?") Consider these follow-ups as reminders that the passive-aggressive person needs.

What to do if all this doesn't work?

If the person persists in being late and not keeping his / her word, try a technique which consist of behaving in the same way, i.e. giving the person a dose of his / her own medicine.

For example:

- Get to a meeting 45 minutes late.
- Pay the person a month late.
- Make a promise, and don't keep it.

Then take time to explain why you did what you did. Ask how s/he felt when you didn't keep your word. Was it pleasant? Would s/he like you to do it again? Well, that's exactly how you felt when...

Then come to a limited and progressive agreement with the person, something along these lines: - 1. If the person has the least inclination to say "No" get him / her to say it immediately. - 2.

Talk things over at least once a month (or once a week...) - 3. If there is any delay, you should be informed immediately.

As with many difficult types, the important thing is to express very clearly how you are affected when the person doesn't keep his / her word, and to reach an agreement together on how to remedy the situation.

Appendix to Chapter 4 V.A.S. Test

For each of the following twelve situations, choose the option you prefer (only one option for each situation).

1. You have to spend six weeks locked up in an underground bomb shelter. You'll have everything necessary for your survival (water, electricity, basic foods, cot and blankets, etc.) You can only bring one singe additional item from the following list with you. Which do you choose?

- A1. A slide projector and a collection of photographs of people, landscapes, works of art, etc.

- B1. A more comfortable bed than the one in the shelter, and a supplementary heater that will provide you with a constant and comfortable temperature.

- C1. A compact disc player and a collection of your favourite music.

2. The thing you like best about a fireplace is:

- A2. Looking at the flames.

- B2. Feeling the heat.

- C2. Hearing the crackling of the wood as it burns.

3. You were invited to a fashionable reception. What you liked most about it was:

- A3. A piece of your favourite music, played by a virtuoso at the end of the evening.

- B3. The extremely comfortable surroundings - soft carpets, sofas, warm light, etc.

- C3. The beauty of the architecture, and the collection of paintings on the walls.

4. You're going out for the first time with someone you find very attractive. What you like most about the person is:

- A4. His / her charming voice.

- B4. The electricity when you touch.

- C4. His / her elegance or physical beauty.

5. What you dislike most in a bed is:

- A5. The way it creaks every time you move.

- B5. The feeling that there are crumbs between the sheets. - C5. That the sheets, although freshly washed, are stained.

6. When giving directions to someone you tend to: - A6. Provide detailed verbal descriptions.

- B6. Make a sketch.

- C6. Accompany the person, or use gestures to point out the right way.

Appendices 7. What would make your work place most pleasant: - A7. Tasteful decor, with lots of plants and colourful prints on the walls. - B7. Background music of your choice, when you want it. - C7. A work table made of some luxurious material that you enjoy touching.

8. Aside from monetary or sentimental value, the gift you'd most prefer receiving would be:

- A8. An article of clothing, in cashmere, fur or silk. - B8. A collection of your favourite music.

- C8. A beautiful painting or print.

9. If you wanted to relax, you'd choose:

- A9. A whirlpool, a massage or a sauna.

- B9. Listening to a tape of relaxing music or words, in a quiet room.

- C9. Contemplating a magnificent landscape.

10. What you find most intolerable about large, overpopulated cities is:

- A10. The crowds of people on the sidewalks and in the subway.

- B10. The ugliness of the grimy buildings, the old torn posters, dirty sidewalks etc.

- C10. The incessant noise of cars and construction.

11. The thing you find most attractive about a river is:

- A11. Refreshing yourself in its cool water, even in the summer heat.

- B11. Closing your eyes and listening to the soothing sound of the water as it rushes by.

- C11. Marvelling at the splendid dance of light on the surface of the water, at the way the water foams as it cascades over the rocks, at the beautiful flowers growing along the riverbank.

12. When you think about something pleasant:

- A12. It's in the form of precise images, alive and in full colour, flowing through your mind.

- B12. You tell yourself about whatever it is, as if you had one, or a number of voices, carrying on a conversation inside your head.

- C12. You recall or anticipate the sensations of pleasure you experienced at that time.

Analysis Table

Circle the choice you made for each of the 12 situations presented (remember - only one choice per situation).

SITUATIONS	TOTAL
Visual	
Auditory	
Sensual	

The sense which collected the most points is probably the one that dominates your perceptions. However, to be absolutely certain, you'd need to do a more detailed analysis. This test is designed solely to make you more aware of the differences between visual, auditory and sensual perceptions in people, and not to measure n those differences accurately.

Visual

Visual people select images from their past, which they then use to interpret what is happening in the present. They don't like staring people in the eyes. They prefer looking around freely, or looking inside their minds for images from the past, or just staring into space, lost in their visions.

Visual people place a lot more emphasis on colours and forms when describing things than do auditory or tactile people. They are usually very sensitive to the colours in their environment, to neatness around them, and to the beauty of landscapes.

Visual people rarely get lost. They retain a mass if interior images, and know how to access these "files" very quickly when the need arises.

Auditory

Auditory people often carry on an inner dialogue with themselves.

They sometimes have trouble making decisions, because these inner voices tend to discuss the issues endlessly, without coming to any clear-cut conclusions. Of course, music lovers are auditory, as are radio announcers.

Auditory people often have pleasant voices, and would choose to go to a concert or listen to some good music when they need to relax.

Tactile (Kinesthetic)

Tactile people "feel" things. They know how to overcome obstacles and resolve conflicts. They often demonstrate conflicting emotions in their own lives: if they don't love a person, they hate them. They insert a lot of pauses when speaking, which gives them time to tune in to their feelings, and establish tactile contact with their surroundings, and with their inner selves.

Olfactory or Gustatory

These two senses also play an important role in defining our perceptions of the world around us, and are more or less developed in different individuals.

However, they practically never become the dominant sense, and that is why they were not included in this test.

Criteria Test

Make TWO choices for each of the eight following situations:

1. Which of the following events would you find most painful?

- A1. Breaking an object which you value a lot beyond repair.

- B1. Losing a bunch of important files, which contain important information on a subject that concerns you, during a move.

- C1. Watching a place you like very much get destroyed (childhood house, village turned into a suburb, park used for construction, etc.).

- D1. Being prevented from doing something you like to do,

Appendices because of lack of time, change of residence, health problems, etc. - E1. Missing an important family or social get together: a wedding, a golden anniversary, an alumnus meeting, etc. - F1. Suddenly losing the friendship of a person you like, for no apparent reason.

2. What is it about past vacations that has made the deepest impression on your mind?

- A2. The people you were with, or whom you met. - B2. The places you discovered, or went back to. - C2. All the things you did that you enjoyed doing.

- D2. The fact that the vacation date coincides with an important event in your life, or that the vacation was the first time that you... (fill in the blank) so that you'll always remember it.

- E2. All the interesting things you learned.

- F2. The beautiful or valuable souvenirs you brought back with you.

3. You have a choice between six jobs: they all offer the same salary, vacation, tenure, and social programmes, and are situated at equal distances from your home. However, each has a particular advantage. Which would you choose?

- A3. This is the first time in the history of the profession that someone with your background and training has been named to the position. The news causes headlines.

- B3. Your office is in an especially prestigious building or environment.

- C3. You will be in charge of one, or a number of activities which you enjoy doing, or which interest you for personal reasons.

- D3. You'll be working closely with an old friend whom you like a lot.

- E3. You'll be provided with very complete information and data, and the latest research techniques.

- F3. You'll be provided with highly sophisticated materials and equipment - the best in your field.

4. For professional reasons, you have to leave home to spend a year in an underdeveloped, tropical country. What worries you the most is:

- A4. The fact that you'll be far from friends and family.

- B4. The fact that the place you're going to offers very few of the comforts you're used to at home, or in the places you usually visit.

- C4. The fact that nothing important ever happens there, and that you'll be totally isolated from any great world events that might take place during your absence.

- D4. The fact that the place is so isolated, you won't have anything to do outside of working hours, and become extremely bored.

- E4. You know nothing about the place you're going to, and you're afraid there will be a serious lack of information of all kinds, both cultural, professional and political.

- F4. The country you're going to doesn't produce anything interesting. If you bring your furnishings with you, the bugs will

Appendices probably eat your carpets, tables and chairs, and the humidity will destroy your paintings and prints.

5. When you think about your childhood, what kinds of memories come most easily to mind?

- A5. The exact names of school friends; the number of stamps you had in your collection; any other precise information about this period in your life.

- B5. Persons who played an important role in your childhood (aside from your parents): friends, neighbours, extended family, teachers...

- C5. Your favourite games, or things you liked to do as a child.

- D5. The toys or other objects you possessed, that gave you a lot of pleasure.

- E5. The place, or places (home, neighbourhood, country village, etc.) where you experienced various important events in your childhood.

- F5. Memorable events (family, political, natural) which you witnessed or took part in.

6. Your dream is to:

- A6. Live amongst warm and communicative people. - B6. Live in a beautiful place.

- C6. Accomplish ten times more than you do now.

- D6. Play a central role in an exceptional event.

- E6. Buy all the little things you want.

- F6. Possess great knowledge, and be universally cultured.

7. The year is 1500 B.C. You are a counsellor to the Pharaoh of Egypt. You are given completely free choice to pick one item, dedicated to posterity, that will be buried with the Pharaoh in his tomb. What would you choose?

- A7. A lifelike and affectionate description of the king's parents, children and friends, describing their qualities, and how devoted they were to their ruler.

- B7. A most beautiful chest made of wood and gold, inset with precious stones, as a testimony to the skill of the artisans in the kingdom.

- C7. A cabinet containing all the medicines known at that time.

- D7. A commemorative plaque depicting the splendour of the Pharaoh's coronation day, and the main events of his reign.

- E7. A painted fresco depicting all the Pharaoh's glorious achievements.

- F7. An empty underground monument, which would serve as a place of meditation for future generations.

8. You learn about the discovery of a tribe of people hither to unknown, in a remote Himalayan valley. The first thing you want to know is:

- A8. How many people there are, what they call themselves, what language they speak, how large their territory is, and any other precise information you can find.

- B8. How this extraordinary discovery took place... on what date, by whom, and under what circumstances.

- C8. What did the tribe's artifacts (pottery, weaving, religious and practical objects, etc.) look like? Will they be exhibited at some time in the near future?

- D8. How do these people, completely isolated for so long, behave? Are they friendly or hostile? Curious about the outside world, or fearful and suspicious? What are the male - female relations like?

- E8. What does their home valley look like? Do they live well? Will it soon be possible to visit them in their natural setting?

- F8. What can be done for them? Is there any kind of organisation you could join to help them?

Analysis Table

Circle your two choices for each of the eight situations:

Situations Total

The two criteria which gain the most points are the ones which are most important to you.

E. Events

For you, life is a succession of events. You can easily remember the dates of things that happened to you. You attach great importance to whatever is a "first" or "last" occasion for you. You seem to intensify circumstances, and herein lies the danger: you may become too preoccupied with isolated events, and forget that "life goes on."

P. Places

The world is made up of places which have special significance for you. You need to know where people you meet come from before you can get to know them. Your environment exerts a strong influence on your behaviour and moods. You form very strong sentimental attachments to certain places. You run the risk of forgetting that man's real "place" is the entire world.

A. Activities

You see the world as a large playing field. To understand someone, you have to know what s/he does in life. When talking about yourself, you gladly tell people what you do, or what you don't do. You sometimes get the feeling you haven't accomplished anything, even though you've been very active all day long. You like work that requires mobility and movement, and you prefer sports to reading. You risk becoming an activity "addict," or a workaholic.

Pe. People

What counts most for you in life is people. You like to be in touch with others, and you're preoccupied with your relationships. When you meet people, you have to know what social group they belongs to, if you have any common friends, etc. in order to relate to them. When you have to make a choice, the most important thing is to know "who" your choice implicates, i.e. what other people are concerned. You may be hindered by your tendency to take things too personally.

I. Information

There's so much to know! You are always looking out for new things to learn in the situations you encounter, and you're very efficient at collecting data. What motivates you the most is your desire to know more, to obtain all kinds of precise information and general data on a host of subjects. The danger for you is that you analyse things too much, instead of living them fully.

O. Objects

For you, the world is full of things that will never be fully explored, classified, preserved and admired. You're very skillful at anything that has to do with objects: organising, classifying, repairing, building, counting, collecting, administrating, conserving, restoring, etc. You'd make a good manager, since you like things to be in order and in good condition. You value the material side of life. You may tend to see living beings a little too much like objects.

Appendix to Chapter 7
Exercise Corrections
A few sample responses:

Exercise on page 173 "If you... really..."

- b. One spouse to another

"If you really loved me, you wouldn't speak to me that way..." Second spouse:

"Do you seriously think I don't love you?"

First spouse:

"It's the way you talk to me that makes me think you don't love me any more."

Second spouse:

"But what you're saying is very serious. Come and sit down for a moment, and let's talk this over. You have to tell me when you started thinking like this."

Comment: You'll notice that the second spouse accepts what the first has said at face value, without getting upset or making any protests (which would lead to an unpleasant scene and other nasty consequences). This way, the bomb is calmly disarmed.

- c. Teacher to student

"If you really wanted to graduate, you wouldn't skip every second class..."

Student:

"But I can assure you that I really do want to graduate."

Teacher:

"In that case, why do you skip classes? It's not the best way to do well in school, believe me..."

At this point, the teacher is probably getting ready to launch into a sermon, which the student does well to interrupt.

Student:

"I understand what you're saying, Sir, and from now on I'll do everything I can to improve my attendance record and get my diploma."

Comment: Instead of making more or less dishonest excuses, the student only responds to the first part of the teacher's statement, providing a way out of an impending conflict.

- d. Doctor to patient:

"If you really wanted to lose weight, you wouldn't eat so many sweets..."

Patient:

"But I really do want top lose weight, Doctor, I can assure you."

Doctor:

"Well, in that case you'll have to pay more attention to your diet. (Here the doctor gives a detailed description of an appropriate diet).

Comment: The patient uses exactly the same manoeuvre as in the previous example. When you feel even slightly in the wrong, as is the case with the student and this patient, this technique is the best way to get yourself out of trouble. You won't have to give any vague, off the cuff explanations, and you assure the other person of your good intentions.

Exercise: "Even you... should..."

- f. Patient to a nurse

"Even a simple nurse should be able to realise when someone is suffering..."

Nurse:

"You know, what you just said is extremely interesting. Certainly a nurse, with all the training s/he has, and with all her professional experience, should be able to recognise when a patient is suffering. You're completely right!"

Comment: The nurse took a deep breath and suppressed her anger, as well as her desire to hit the patient over the head with a bead pan and say something like, "With patients like you, it's a wonder nurses like me aren't all in the loony bin!"

She pretended not to understand that she was being insulted, and totally ignored the sarcasm in the patient's voice. She refused to show that she was upset, and created the impression that she was really interested.

Patient:

"Oh, well... yes, obviously..."

Nurse:

"Good. Now how about taking your temperature?"

- g. Child to mother:

"Mother, even you should be able to understand that I need some new summer clothes..."

Mother:

"It's quite popular among contemporary adolescents to think that their parents are complete idiots, incapable of understanding anything. But don't you worry about it, you'll get over it in a few years."

Comment: Once again the intended victim has used the element of surprise to turn things around. The technique consists of shifting the attack to an impersonal level. It usually succeeds in this kind of situation.

Child:

"Mother, you're making fun of me. That's not what I was talking about..."

Mother:

"Really? Well what were you talking about. Come and explain it to me, so that I can understand."

- h. Husband to wife

"Even you should be able to learn how to drive this car properly..."

Wife:

"Some men actually do think their wives are idiots, but I'm surprised to see that you think that way too."

Comment: This is still the same technique of depersonalising the attack. The manoeuvre is non-violent, and ends on a kind of compliment: the husband doesn't belong to the category of crass, unfeeling men who insult their wives in this way. The last part of the sentence implies that the husband may be having some kind of a hard time, or that his comment is a simple lapse of character. The wife generously offers him the benefit of the doubt.

If you find it impossible to avoid counter-attacking, for example if the husband becomes excessively abusive and condescending, and the wife wants to put a stop to the insults once and for all, she can always transform her little compliment into a cutting remark, as we saw earlier on:

Wife:

"The notion that women are incapable of driving is common to men of a certain age, dear. But don't worry, it's not serious."

Comment: "...of a certain age" is the crucial phrase in the sentence. It could, of course, be replaced by variations such as: ...of your generation; ... in your situation; ...of your intelligence; ...of your profession, etc.

Exercise: appealing to emotions (pg.179)

- j. Husband to wife:

"Why do you always try to make me look stupid?" Wife:

"But... listen, I have an idea! We'll have a party, invite all our friends. But first you'll make a list of all the things you want me to talk about, and also what you don't want me to mention, so that I don't make you feel stupid."

Comment: The usual technique, in such situations, is to offer a suggestion that will remedy the complaint, but a suggestion that you know the other person will refuse. This is exactly what the wife does here. The husband's reaction is predictable.

Husband:

"That's ridiculous. It would be completely bizarre..."

Wife:

"All right, let's forget it. It wasn't such a great idea anyway." Comment: The subject is closed for the moment. The husband would feel ridiculous insisting in the face of such adamant good will. - k. Parent to child

"Can't you ever do anything to please me?" Child:

"How about trying something? From now on, I'll come and check my homework with you every night. And you can come to all the parent - teacher meetings, so you can get to know my teachers. That way, I'll get good marks, and you can say that I did something to please you."

Comment: Once again, the technique consists of suggesting something that will probably scare the other person off. The child knows that his / her parent is already overloaded with things to do, and won't agree to this proposal.

Parent:

"Uh, well, let's talk about it next week, when I have some time..."

Credits

Illustration couverture : © Content Factory

© IAB 2008 — Tous droits réservés

www.ingramcontent.com/pod-product-compliance
Lightning Source LLC
Chambersburg PA
CBHW031146020426
42333CB00013B/528